"First Abraham, our courier, appeared, riding a fine Arab horse." Page 38.

PHILIP

IN

PALESTINE.

EDITED BY M. A. EDWARDS.

PHILADELPHIA:
JAMES S. CLAXTON,
SUCCESSOR TO WM. S. & ALFRED MARTIEN,
606 CHESTNUT STREET.
1865.

Stereotyped and Printed by Alfred Martien.

CONTENTS.

INTRODUCTION.

My Young Friends:—

When you are introduced to a new acquaintance, you feel a desire to know something about him beyond the mere name. I think, then, you will like these letters better if I, the Editor, tell you something about the boy who wrote them. I shall be very brief, for his life was a smooth and common-place one, though he, like other boys, thought it full of important incidents, and sometimes felt that it was full of troubles.

Philip Conway was the only son of a wealthy merchant of Philadelphia. He lost his mother when he was an infant, which was the one misfortune his life had yet known. Her place had been supplied, as much as a mother's can be, by his aunt. His father retired from business when Philip was very young, and, from that time, devoted himself to his son. He not only sent Philip to a good school, but took care that he learned his lessons and understood them. Under this training, Philip became a studious boy. He was fond of reading, and, as his father was a religious man, he early directed his son's attention to the Bible, which children will find a very entertaining as well as instructive book, if they once get into the habit of reading it.

Philip found it so at any rate; and, though it may seem strange to most boys, he actually knew as much about David, the giant-killer, as he did about Jack, the giant-killer; the account of the strange wanderings of the children of Israel, the wonderful exploits of Samson, and the miracles of Elijah and Elisha, were oftener in his mind, and seemed to him more entertaining and wonderful than the bewitching, but false miracles and wonders of the Arabian Nights. He was as well acquainted with the sweet and simple Ruth as with little Nell; and the romantic story of Queen Esther had for him a greater charm than that of a heroine of a novel, because he knew it to be true.

When Philip was fifteen years old, Mr. Conway determined to visit Palestine. This had long been a great desire with him, made stronger, just then, by the fact that Mr. Hamilton, his most intimate friend, had made arrangements for a journey to that country. What to do with Philip he did not know, for he and his son had never been parted, when the boy settled the matter by proposing that he should go too. After a little hesitation, Mr. Conway consented, for he thought what his son would learn in his travels would probably be of greater advantage to him than the year's schooling he would lose.

But to this consent a condition was annexed, and that was, that Philip should regularly write to his friend, Harry Blake, a true and faithful account of all that he should see, and all that he could learn about the country and people of Palestine. The reason why this was made a condition will probably be as apparent to my readers as it was to Philip himself. This he readily agreed to, for he rather liked letter-writing, and he loved Harry Blake very much indeed.

Harry was the eldest of a large family. He

and Philip were near neighbors. They were of the same age; had the same tastes; were in the same classes at school, and enjoyed the same games. It is, therefore, not surprising that they were fast friends. Caroline, who is occasionally mentioned in these pages, was a sister of Harry's, a little younger than himself.

Hartley Graham was a youth, some nineteen or twenty years old. When the visit to Palestine was decided upon, he requested permission to make one of the party. Mr. Conway was pleased to have Hartley with them. He was a pleasant and intelligent companion, and Philip's father felt that he would be a connecting link between the boy of fifteen and the grave, middle-aged men.

So the four left America in the month of September, 18—, and they had a very delightful journey through the Holy Land, as you will see if you read these letters.

The only alterations made in the letters by the Editor, is that of leaving out the allusions to home incidents, and the numerous messages Philip sent to everybody, old or young, that he knew. These, though no doubt pleasant enough to Harry, would not interest the general reader.

PHILIP IN PALESTINE.

I.

BEIRUT, Nov. 20, 18—.

MY DEAR HARRY:—

At last I am actually in Palestine! I scarcely realize it yet, for, although this is the queerest place I ever saw—not at all like Philadelphia—yet I see a great many things that remind me of home, for I am staying in the Frank quarter of the town, which is inhabited by Europeans. When I get out into the wild country, and among the little Arab villages, no doubt I shall have many strange things to tell you.

We left Alexandria about two weeks ago, in a steamboat! To come to the Holy Land in a steamboat seemed to me to be out of all propriety, and I wanted to come in the same kind of ship that St. Paul sailed in to Rome; but father only laughed at me, and said he thought I would find the steamboat more comfortable. It had the advantage in point of speed at any rate, for we were only forty hours from Alexandria to this place.

We were landed above the city, at a bare, dreary-looking house, called the Lazaretto, where we were compelled to stay five days in quarantine. This was a very dull time.

My amusements were watching the arrival and departure of the few vessels which come here, reading, and sleeping. On the fifth day, the authorities, being satisfied that we had not brought any contagious disease to their city, permitted us to come into the town. We are staying with Mr. and Mrs. Marshall, who are friends of Mr. Hamilton's. They are very nice old people, and have a house in the Frank quarter of the city. But, as I said before, I don't *feel* that I am in Palestine yet, as I have never associated this place with the country at all. This is not a Bible city. By that I mean that it is not mentioned in the Bible. It is said to be very ancient, however, although nobody seems to know when it was founded. It is probable that it was one of the cities of the Phœnicians, for along this coast was their country. It is a very beautiful city. If you will go with me to the top of the house, you can get a first-rate view of it. I mean, of course, go with me in imagination, but I wish you could be with me in reality.

It seems quite natural to me now to talk about the housetop, but it was very strange at first. The houses here, and throughout the whole country, have flat roofs, and these are more frequented by the people than the porches are with us. It is the coolest part of the house, and is a delightful promenade, especially in the morning and evening; and, as there are very few windows looking into the street from these houses, you have to go to the housetops, if you want to see what is going on. The people spend a great deal of time there—attend to their business, entertain their visitors, and sometimes even sleep there.

They also use them for drying clothes, in the city, and in the villages the farmers dry their figs and raisins there. So you see, the housetop is the most important part of the house, and I offered you no disrespect by inviting you to go there with me. Our roof has a stone battlement all around it, so you need not be afraid of falling off. All houses are not protected in the same way; but the Jewish people were commanded to build battlements to their roofs, that "they brought not blood upon their house."* The housetops are often covered with vines, which must be very agreeable in the summer time.

Just imagine that I have been telling you all that while we were going up-stairs. Now we are safely at the housetop (where, by the way, I am writing this letter), let us look around us. First look to the north, where the Mediterranean is sparkling in the sunlight. It is a quiet sea, almost tideless, and of a light blue color at this distance, except that long waving line of white light, where it breaks against the rocks. It forms a very pretty bay at this part of the coast, on which the city is situated, which is called the Bay of St. George. If you look to the southeast, you will find what, at first sight, seems to be another sea, with waves of glistening whiteness. But if you look closer, you will see it is a dense mass of silvery-looking foliage. These are olive groves, said to be the largest and most productive in Syria. On the southwest is a broad belt of loose sand. Between the olive groves and the sand, are beautiful pine forests, which have been planted there, for the pine is not native to these plains. There are other trees in this lovely plain, but they do not grow in such dense groves as the olives and pines. We have orange, lemon,

* Deut. xxii. 8.

mulberry, figs, almond, apricot, sycamore, prickly oak, and some others which are totally unknown to you. Now look to the east and northeast. The scenery is much wilder. There are the mountains, very steep and rugged-looking from here, and yet their sides are dotted with villages, churches, and convents, and covered with pine forests. And, beyond these, a little further in the distance, is glorious old Lebanon! When I look there, I feel that I am really in the Holy Land.

These mountains are much higher than I had any idea of. The highest peak is 9310 feet high. They look dazzlingly white from here when the sunlight falls upon them; on cloudy days they look like masses of white clouds piled up against the sky. I thought this appearance was caused by snow, but father says only the very highest peaks are covered with snow; their whiteness is owing to the white limestone rocks. Hence the name "Lebanon," which is the Hebrew for "White Mountain." Father also tells me that the sides of these mountains are covered with villages, and cultivated to the very top. I am sure no one would suspect such a thing, looking at the mountains from this place. They seem to be composed of great masses of naked, whitish-looking rock, cut up by ravines, which run down to the plain. This appearance must be owing to the rocks being very steep—the villages are hidden behind them. The way these rocks are cultivated is this: they build terraces with great labor, and cover them with soil, which is carried there.

I had always thought there was but one range of Lebanon mountains, and am quite surprised to find there are *two.* They are known as Lebanon and Anti-Lebanon. The two ranges meet near Mount Hermon. Their shape is somewhat like the letter V, only one limb should be made longer than the other. The left limb of the letter would represent Lebanon, the right Anti-Lebnaon. Mount Hermon would be almost at the point of the V. The valley between the two ranges is called Cœle-Syria. All south of Hermon is Palestine, or Holy Land, and all north and east is Syria. (So you see I am not in Palestine proper, though this part of the country is often called Palestine.) The country of the Phœnicians lay along this coast. Their territory was not more than eleven miles wide, and extended southward only as far as Mount Hermon. What a little country for such a great people! Pennsylvania would be a mighty empire by the side of it! All this country was included in the Land of Promise; but, as you well know, the Jews never obtained possession of the whole land promised to them. We expect to travel among the Lebanon mountains some of these days, when I can give you more particular descriptions. I give you this general view of them, because I expect I shall often mention them, as they can be seen all along our route. I am very anxious to climb up Sunnin, which I look at every day, lifting its lofty white head into the air. It is one of the highest of the peaks, and not far from Beirut.

And now, after this long wandering among the mountains, we will return to our housetop view. Just outside the city took place the famous fight between St. George and the dragon. We can look down on the very spot, and if we were there I would show you the well down which the dragon was thrown. I don't believe you know this story. I never heard it until since I have been here, and I will tell it to you in my own fashion:—

Once upon a time, then—a very great many years ago I think it must have been—when some parts of the earth were infested with terrible and fiery monsters, a great dragon inhabited this part of the Mediterranean Sea. This dragon was as large as six good-sized elephants put together. He had the head of a lion, the body of a fish, and the tail of a scorpion—all greatly enlarged of course. His mouth was so big that when it was open you could have driven a carriage and four into it with great ease, and had room to turn round and drive out again—if he would only let you. This was all awful enough, to be sure; but what made him still more horrible was, that when he got angry, which was pretty often, flames of fire gushed out o' his mouth. This portly and respectable gentleman was in the habit of coming out of the sea at a certain time during the day (nobody knew exactly what hour he would fix upon), and taking a leisurely stroll about the country; for this kind of animal I have described lives equally well in fire, water, or on the earth, and is as often seen in one element as in the other. He seemed to think this a good opportunity to take his dinner, which he did in a manner more agreeable to himself than to the public at large. He thought nothing of gobbling up a whole village full of people, and, if a stray traveller chanced in his way, he would snap him up in a twinkling.

The people soon found that only one person could play at this game, and the country was presently deserted by its inhabitants, who flocked into the great city, which stood where Beirut does now, only it had a different name,

But they might almost as well have been swallowed by the dragon, for the city was so crowded that a dreadful pestilence broke out in it; and, as there was no one left in the country to cultivate the fields they were all in danger of famine. And then all trade and commerce was at end, for no ship dared come there, because of the dragon.

At last, in some way (I am sure I don't know how), the dragon was persuaded to listen to reason, and a bargain was struck between him and the people. He promised to behave himself in as quiet and respectable a manner as it is possible for a dragon to do. He agreed to limit his promenades to one particular part of the shore—never to disturb the city—not to harm anybody he might chance to meet—and not to molest the ships. In return for all this the people agreed to furnish him his dinner every day. Now you might suppose that this would be an impossible thing to do, judging from the amount of food he had been in the habit of taking; but it seems he had, all at once, grown very delicate in his appetite, and nothing would serve him for dinner but a tender and beautiful young maiden.

And so, every morning, at sunrise, all the beautiful young girls in the city were assembled, and lots cast as to who should go out to be offered to the dragon. The unfortunate one on whom the lot fell, having taken a sad farewell of all she loved, was led out to a place near the city and fastened to a stake in the sands, where she remained until the dragon chose to come and make a meal of her. I think, Harry, the ugly girls must have thanked their stars at that time!

Well, this went on for some time, and the pretty girls were getting rather scarce in the city, when the great St. George happened this way. I can't stop to tell you now who this St. George was, and, in fact, I don't know much about him, only that he was a very good, and wonderfully strong and courageous man—like Great Heart, in Pilgrim's Progress, I suppose. He was very indignant when he heard all that the dragon had been doing, and declared he would kill him and deliver the earth from such a cruel monster. So the next morning, when the beautiful young maiden was led out of the city, he went with her. He was clad in armor from head to foot and had a mighty shield, and a sword that had slain many an enemy. He rode a splendid steed that was afraid of no creature. When the dragon came out for his dinner there was a terrible fight, which lasted many hours—the beautiful young maiden looking on and praying for her champion. Of course St. George killed the dragon; but I don't know exactly in what way. The body of the dragon was thrown down the well I pointed out to you, and St. George bore the fair maiden in triumph to the city, which was filled with rejoicing for many days and nights.

To end the story in the usual way, I should say that St. George married the beautiful maiden, but I am pretty sure that he did not. The well is still here, as I told you; but I don't believe that with the most patient digging we would be able to find a single bone of the mighty dragon. You know it all happened so very long ago.

That was a long digression. If I stray about in this way I shall never get on.

You must not leave the housetops without a glance down at the city. You see the houses are high and built of stone. They are very comfortable, at least those I have been in. But their walls look dark and gloomy. They have so few windows, that is, in the old city, within the walls; we live outside of the walls. Beirut, they say, has grown very much within the last thirty years, and the largest part of the city is outside of the walls. It is the prettiest part, also, for the houses are surrounded by pretty gardens. The dwellings of the Franks are in this part of the city. Europeans and Americans are all called Franks here, without distinction of country.

And now I will show you something curious—something you never saw in any city before. It is the wall which surrounds the original city. See! it is dark and high, with little narrow slits in it. That square, turret-like building is a gate. The part you see is a large, square room, the gateway is below. In reading the Old Testament, you remember we used to think it strange that people went to the gates for pleasure, or to transact business and to hold courts of justice. But if you would go with me to the gate I have just been pointing out to you, you would not think it strange that people would like to spend a great deal of time there. You enter through an arched way into a large vaulted place, cool and shady, and when you recollect that everybody who goes in and out of the city had to pass through these gates, you can easily imagine it was the very place to see all that was going on and hear the news. They are often used now for the same purposes they were in olden times.

But the streets of Beirut! O, Harry! the very meanest street in Philadelphia is a magnificent avenue compared with these. They are positively only eight feet wide; and, when I tell you that the houses on each side are fifty or sixty feet high, and generally with perfectly blank walls, you can judge how miserably dark and dismal are the streets. But that is not the worst of them. They have no sidewalks, and the gutters are in the middle! They are miserably paved, and the walking is disagreeable enough when the street is perfectly clear of everything. But when it happens that a long train of camels and donkeys come along (and this is always happening), you have to "run the gauntlet" round the animals, and under them—in every direction but *over* them—unless a friendly recess or open door receives you. The drivers scream out at the top of their lungs some words which are Arabic for "Look sharp!" and "Take care!" which is very polite of them to be sure.

You will wonder how carriages get along in such streets, and the fact is they don't get along at all. There are no carriages here, or vehicles of any kind, and I am told there are none anywhere in Syria. Is it not wonderful that people can get along without them? But from what I have seen and heard of the various inhabitants of Syria I don't believe they like to get along, especially in anything that goes very fast. They have pretty much the same ideas, manners and customs their forefathers had eighteen hundred years ago. This suits us very well, as we shall get a better idea of what the country was during the time of our Saviour. The people say there are no good roads in Syria, which is the reason they cannot use wheels. Why don't they make good roads then? They must have been good a long time ago, for, in the Bible, we read of wagons and chariots.

One curious thing about this city is, that all of the same trade live in the same street. Thus we have Saddler's street, Blacksmith's street, &c.

Gas is unheard of here. The streets are not lighted at all. The shops are all closed at dusk, and the streets are silent and deserted until morning. If you wish to go anywhere at night you will find it necessary to take a lantern with you.

This city contains forty thousand inhabitants, and a curious and mixed people they are: Americans, Europeans of all nations, Jews, Turks, Arabs, and I don't know how many others. You have twenty different languages around you at once.

Some curious sights will greet you also. Here, you look into a barber's shop, where a man has just had every particle of hair shaved off his head! There, you see a woman with a long, thick veil on, entirely concealing her face. There are two holes cut in the veil for her to see through. There again, are some men on a roof, saying their prayers. They are Moslems, and the confusion around them, and the public place they are in, does not seem to distract them. What curious motions they go through! They fall on their knees; they touch their foreheads to the ground; they sit; they stand erect—all the time repeating their prayers, or passages from the Koran, as fast as they can. They often do not understand what they are saying. In front of that mosque sits a letter-writer. His business is to write letters for those who cannot write themselves, and their number is not small. He sits cross-legged on a cushion, and spreads his paper on his lap (sometimes he has an ink-stand on a little table). His ink-horn hangs at his girdle, and his pen is made from a kind of reed.

I think I have told you all that would interest you in regard to Beirut. We have been here a week, and have been making preparations for the great journey we have before us. As there are no wagons all our baggage must be carried by mules and camels. It will require several of these animals to take it all, for we have to carry tents, household furniture, and everything with us. The drivers will be Arabs.

Father and Mr. Hamilton have English horses, but Hartley and I preferred Arab ponies. Mine is a little beauty, and very gentle. He knows me already. He is said to be very sure-footed; I don't know about that, but he travels very fast—on a good road he will go a mile in four minutes. I call him Saladin. He is one of my heroes, and as I shall visit the scenes of his exploits, I thought it a suitable name for my pony.

Our courier is named Ibrahim, which is an odd name, but common enough here. He is a very grave and dignified-looking Arab, and has travelled with Franks so many times that he knows all their ways, and what they like to eat, and what they like to see. His business is to attend to everything generally, so that we may not be bothered thinking of small matters. The attendants are all under his command, and he is the guide. He transacts all the business, pays all the bills, and is very careful that no one shall cheat his employers but himself. But Ibrahim is considered very honest—for an Arab. He speaks English after a fashion of his own, but we can understand him.

Our preparations are nearly complete, and I hope we will soon commence our journey, for I am getting impatient.

Your affectionate friend,

PHILIP.

II.

BEIRUT, Dec. 1, 18—.

MY DEAR HARRY:—

You see we are here yet. We were all ready to start when Hartley was taken sick. He is better now, and will be able to travel in a couple of days. Father advised me to while away the time by writing to you again, and telling you about the different races and sects who inhabit this country. He says you will have a better understanding of my letters if you know of the different people and religions. He has taken a great deal of pains to teach me all these things since we have been in this city, and, as I see the people all around me, I have a better understanding of them, and of their religious beliefs, than I ever had before.

I told you of the division of this country into Syria, Cœle-Syria, and Palestine. The whole of it has, for a great many years, been under the rule of the Moslems, and a very bad rule it seems to be. The entire population is to be found in the towns and villages, it being dangerous to live in the open country, on account of the lawlessness and violence of the wandering Arabs; the Government, though powerful enough to oppress the people, does not seem to have the power or inclination to protect them.

There are five different Mohammedan sects and nine Christian sects, and as these are always quarrelling among each other, and the bitterest hate exists among them, you need not wonder that every few years everything is put in confusion, and the whole country visited by anarchy and civil war. I believe the Protestants have never taken any part in these numerous quarrels. They are so few in number, that they are not regarded as of much importance by the other sects.

I have the numbers of each sect, but they are not *exact*, as the census is not taken regularly here, as in our country. As the Mohammedans have the rule, I will begin with them.

I have often been very much confused by the names, Mohammedans, Moslems, Musselmen, Islams, and Turks, but I have found out that they are all different names for the same things. They all believe in one God, and that Mohammed was the Prophet of God, and for this reason they have always been called Mohammedans. Turkey is the chief seat of this religion, although it is spread through all Eastern countries, and therefore Mohammedans everywhere are often called Turks, although the name is properly applied only to a native of Turkey. The name Moslem was given to Mohammedans by the Crusaders, and we have retained it ever since. They call themselves Mussulmen; to the faith they believe they give the name "Islam," which means "the faith," (in the same way that we call the Word of God "Bible," or "the Book," to show that it is above all other books;) hence they are sometimes called Islams.

I said there were five Mohammedan sects, but, properly speaking, there is but one; the other four are considered heresies. The Mohammedans proper, or the Moslems, as they are more frequently called in this country, number 800,000. They hate Christians, and call them dogs, or infidels. They allow Christians to stay in the country, and have their own churches and form of worship; partly because they are afraid of European nations, but chiefly, I suspect, because of the immense amount of money they get from the pilgrims. The Moslems are found all over the country everywhere, and constitute the mass of the people, except in Lebanon. Notwithstanding their hatred of Christians, they believe the Saviour to have been a great prophet—the greatest, next to Mohammed! They hold the tombs of the patriarchs and of David in great reverence, and will not let Christians look at them. They believe in the resurrection, and a final judgment.

The Druses are mostly found on Lebanon. They number about 100,000. They were formerly very powerful in the mountains, but now they are inferior to the Maronites (a Christian sect), and many of the great Druse lords have become Maronites. They are a very curious people, and this was their origin: About eight hundred years ago there was a tyrannical ruler of Egypt, who was persuaded by an artful Persian to call himself a god. Soon after the new god disappeared mysteriously, murdered by the Persian, probably, who took care that the people should believe he had been translated to heaven. This Persian, Hakim, then said the god had left a book suspended at the door of a great mosque; and there the book was found! This book the Druses reverence as their Bible. If you ask them what they believe, they won't tell you, but pretend to believe as you do. They hold their meetings in secret, and it is said they have some horrible ceremonies, but that is only suspicion. One of their doctrines we know: that the soul, when it leaves the body, goes into some animal, say a horse; when the horse dies, it goes into a donkey, maybe; then into an owl, &c. Pretty doctrine, is n't it? It may be a comfort to a Druse to think of becoming a donkey, but it would not be to me.

Of the Nusairiyeh, who live among the northern mountains, there are 150,000. Very little is known about them, as they also keep their religion a secret.

The Metaweleys inhabit the district south of Lebanon, and east of Tyre. Their mode of worship is much like the Mohammedans. They are 150,000 in number.

The Ismaelites have a secret, mystical religion. They are now but few in numbers—about 20,000. They are the descendants of the people called Assassins in the time of the Crusaders. They were at one time very numerous in Syria. The founder was a Persian, named Hassan, called "Old Man of the Mountain," because his castle was situated on a very lofty hill. Around his palace this prince caused beautiful gardens and pavilions to be built. He had powders secretly administered to young men whom he selected as converts. These powders threw them into a profound sleep. While in this condition they were conveyed into the gardens, and, on awaking, were regaled with everything that could delight the senses, and were constantly charmed with new delights. After they had passed some days in this manner, they were again put to sleep, and carried back. They were then told that these were only foretastes of the delights they would forever experience, if in this life they remained faithful subjects of Hassan. These young men made converts of others, and thus his power was extended. Their sole idea of religion seemed to be blind obedience to Hassan. As his commands were generally for them to kill somebody whom he did not like, the Crusaders gave them the name of Assassins.

Henry, Count of Champagne, paid a visit to the chief of the Assassins, and was received with distinguished honors. The chief led him to all parts of his palace, and finally conducted him up a very lofty tower, upon every step of which stood men clothed in white. "I do not suppose," said the chief to Henry, "that you have any subjects as obedient as mine." At the same time he made a sign with his hand, when two men threw themselves from the top of the tower, and expired instantly. The chief then said:—"If you desire it, at the least signal from me, any of these men will throw themselves down in the same manner; and if you have any enemy who aims at your crown, address yourself to me, and my servants will soon relieve you of all anxiety, by poignarding him."

A powerful Sultan once sent to Hassan, and demanded the surrender of his castles. Hassan ordered one of his servants into his presence, and ordered him to kill himself, which he immediately did. He then told another to throw himself from the top of a lofty tower, and his order was obeyed. He then said to the ambassador, "Repeat to your master what you have seen, and tell him I have 60,000 men at my command, who are as devoted and obedient as these." The Sultan troubled him no further. Such were the Assassins at the time of the Crusaders. They are now greatly reduced in number, and no longer have a terrible Hassan at their head.

The Christian sects are Greeks, Greek Catholics, Maronites, Syrians, or Jacobites, Syrian Catholics, Armenians, Armenian Catholic, Latins, and Protestants.

The most widely-spread of these are the Greeks, so called because they profess the Greek faith, and belong to the Greek Church. They are Arabs, like the other Arabs of the country. They use the Arabic language in their worship. Their bishops are Greek by birth, but their priests are native, and are chosen by the people. They are usually married, and work at some trade. They are very ignorant, but that don't prevent them from teaching school. They teach, and work at their trade at the same time, and vary this by attending to their parish duties and preaching. At all events, nobody can accuse them of being idle.

Greek Catholics are very much like the Greeks, only they acknowledge the authority of the Pope of Rome, and believe in purgatory. They have a college and printing press, and are among the wealthiest inhabitants of Syria, and possess great influence.

I don't know how many members the above churches have.

The Maronites are native Syrians, and number about 200,000. They are found in cities and large towns, but their home may be said to be in the mountains of Lebanon, where they have succeeded in getting the upper hand of the Druses. They are devoted to the Pope of Rome, and completely under the dominion of their priests. They only take the bread in communion, but in other respects, I believe, are not much like the Romish Church. They have a college which is said to be pretty good, for a Syrian college. They have fifty convents.

The Latins are Roman Catholics. They amount only to a few hundreds, and are mostly persons connected with the convents and holy places in Palestine. In some instances the Greeks and Latins occupy the same churches, and fight and quarrel in the most shameful manner.

The other Christian sects are unimportant. There are not more than fifty thousand in all.

Then there are the wandering Arab tribes, who are to be found everywhere, but cannot be counted, because they are always going about. They are Moslems.

Beside all these, there are the Jews, who number about 25,000. I believe they are only to be found in a few of the cities. Jerusalem contains seven thousand of them. The few that are in the country are scarcely tolerated, and seem generally to be despised by their neighbors. And yet this is all their own country! their "Promised Land!" How bitterly they must feel when they think of it! Since I have been here, I have often repeated to myself a little poem I learned some years ago, when I was a little boy:—

THE WILD GAZELLE.

The wild gazelle on Judah's hills
  Exulting yet may bound;
And drink from all the living rills
  That gush on holy ground;
Its airy step and glorious eye
May glance in tameless transport by.

A step as fleet, an eye more bright,
  Hath Judah witnessed there;
And o'er her scenes of lost delight
  Inhabitants more fair;
The cedars wave o'er Lebanon,
But Judah's statelier maids are gone.

More blest each palm that shades those plains,
  Than Israel's scattered race,
For, taking root, it there remains,
  In melancholy grace;
It cannot quit its place of birth,
It will not live in other earth.

But we must wander witheringly,
  In other lands to die,
And where our father's ashes be,
  Our own must never lie;
Our temple hath not left a stone,
And mockery sits on Salem's throne.

But they will be restored to this land, for God hath said it, and he will perform it. The time will come when the proud Moslem will be seen no more in all this country, and the hosts of the Jews, gathered from the east and the west, from every nation and clime, shall take possession of Jerusalem. I would like now, from this housetop, to watch the long procession filing over the hills and plains, with the cross and the name of Christ inscribed on their banners. Your affectionate friend,

PHILIP.

III.

SIDON, Dec. 4, 18—.

MY DEAR HARRY:—

We are still in the country of the Phœnicians. This was one of their chief cities. But what makes it more interesting to us is, that it is a Bible city. Father found for me all the places where it is mentioned. It is first spoken of in the tenth chapter of Genesis. Only think how old it is! It has been destroyed and rebuilt a great many times since then. In the nineteenth chapter of the same book it is mentioned as the boundary of the land promised to Zebulon. In Joshua it is called *great*—three thousand years ago! In Judges the Zidonians are spoken of as oppressing the people of Israel. In Kings they are said to have been skilful in hewing timber. In Chronicles they are mentioned as carrying cedar wood to David.

But the city has a still nearer interest. It was here that our Lord met with the Canaanitish woman, and healed her daughter;* and Paul

* Matt. xv. 21–27.

and his friends visited this place on their way to Italy.*

It is a small city now—not more than ten thousand inhabitants all told. But, before giving you a description of the city, I must tell you about our ride from Bierut to this place. The distance is twenty-seven miles, but we were twelve hours performing the journey, and it was dark when we reached the gates. There was so much to see, and everybody had so much to say about all that was seen, that we loitered very much on the road. It was the most interesting ride I have ever taken in my life, and it was over the very worst road I ever saw. Hartley says it is one of the best roads in Syria, but I hope he is only joking.

We left Beirut at the first peep of dawn. Mr. Hamilton and father mounted on their horses, and Hartley and I on our ponies, dashed out of the gate in fine style, and then drew up the side of the road to watch our little caravan file out. First Ibrahim, our courier, appeared, riding on a fine Arab horse. A general commanding an army could not have looked more important than he did. Then two poor little patient donkeys came out on a half trot; then four great awkward camels stalked out, one step of their's being about

* Acts xxvii. 3.

equal to ten of the donkeys. These six animals carry on their backs our wardrobes, household furniture, tents, etc., etc. Their drivers are all Arabs, and are very picturesque looking with their loose flowing abas (a kind of cloak), gay turbans and red shoes. Positively red shoes!

The day was clear and beautiful; the air soft, without being too warm—very much like our May days. After leaving the gardens of Beirut we rode through a pine grove for some little time. Through the trees we caught glimpses of the sea, and occasionally we would meet with a stately and beautiful palm tree. These trees are tall and slender; the trunks are smooth and very straight. The leaves grow in a great cluster on the top. They are very long, and of a beautiful vivid green. The fruit grows in clusters, and is said to be of a rich golden yellow, and almost transparent when ripe. This don't answer very well to the description of dates as we have seen them in America, for they are very dark and all matted together. I shall have an opportunity of tasting the fresh fruit in its season.

We next passed through the great olive groves I mentioned in my first letter. They are the largest in Syria. These trees are very valuable property. A full-grown tree yields from ten to fifteen gallons of oil in season, and an acre of them will yield a crop worth a hundred dollars. These groves near Beirut have a great many different owners, hundreds of people own trees there—some only own *one* tree. And yet there is no fence or any landmark to divide one man's property from another. You may wonder how they manage matters in the gathering season, and I will tell you the process. Early in the autumn the berries begin to drop off the trees themselves. They remain on the ground sometime, not even the owners are allowed to pick them up. They are guarded by watchmen, appointed by the authorities. At the proper time the Governor issues a proclamation that all who own trees can go and gather the berries which have fallen. In good seasons this is done two or three times. When the rainy season commences a proclamation is issued for the *shaking* of the olives. Then every man has to look around him pretty sharply and take care of his own; for everybody, men, women and children, flock to the olive groves, climb the trees, shake down the fruit, and carry off all they can get. But even this is not the last gathering, for there will always be some berries left; and these the very poor, who own no trees at all, are allowed to glean. All these customs have remained unchanged since the Israelites first took possession of the land, as we know from accounts in the Bible of the gathering and shaking of the olive.

Although this tree is so valuable, a person who plants an olive must have a great stock of patience on hand, for the tree does not produce any berries at all until it is seven years of age, and the crop is not worth much until the tree is ten or fifteen years old! But, after it once begins, it continues to bear fruit for hundreds of years, for the olive is of longer life than even the oak. It requires but little care to cultivate it, and, if entirely neglected for fifty years, will revive again with a little attention, and be as fruitful as before. None of these trees were very tall, though some of them were very large. They are generally twisted into strange shapes. Some of them were so old they had scarcely a leaf on them, and yet these produce a large crop of berries every year.

These olive groves all have to be *made*, for the wild olive is not good. They either graft the wild olives with grafts from good olives, or else cut off slips that have been grafted and plant them. In this way all that splendid grove was made. The olive leaves are of a light green color, with an under surface of white. The blossoms are small and white, and said to be innumerable in the blossoming season. The trees are almost enveloped in them, like a covering of snow; but not more than one in a hundred of them ever comes to anything.

Olive oil you are familiar with, and the berries also. I don't like the berries at all, but the people here are extravagantly fond of them. Poor people often eat nothing else with their bread, and they use the oil for cooking nearly everything they eat, beside depending upon it for light; and all their soap is made from it. So much for the olives.

After leaving them we passed over a sandy waste. This sand is thrown up by the waves on the beach, and carried by the winds up the shore. They say it is constantly spreading inland. The sand is yellow and piled up in ridges, some of them twenty feet high. By this time we all felt like taking a lunch, and concluded to stop at an inn near by. Inns are here called khans. This one was Khan Khuldeh. It was a very poor, bare-looking house, and there we drank some Arab coffee, as strong as it could be made, and black as ink, with no milk in it. I drank it, with a great many wry faces, for I have made up my mind to be satisfied with what I can get.

We soon after reached the river Damur. Before crossing it we rode up the mountain side a little way to look at the sarcophagi, which are numerous thereabouts. These are stone coffins, and of all sizes, from two to eight feet long. Some are cut out in the rock, others out of hewn stone. They have heavy lids, but no inscriptions on them. There is nothing inside of them, for they have been where they now are hundreds and hundreds of years. For a great many years the inhabitants of the country have been breaking them up for building stones or to burn in the limekilns, and yet there are hundreds of coffins there now. I wonder who was buried in them! Father says he cannot even guess.

We forded the Damur, which was only a shallow stream, but it is subject to floods. We rested awhile under the oleanders and weeping willows on the bank, and then had a pic-nic dinner. It was very romantic.

Directly after leaving the river we passed an Arab encampment. It was not such a pretty sight as I expected it would be. The tents were of a dark brown color, almost black. The Arabs were lounging about, looking very lazy and very dirty. Greasy-looking children stared at us and mangy dogs barked at us.

Then we passed a huge sand-hill, where we could see great stones. Mr. Hamilton told me that was all that was left of what was a great city ages ago. The city was called Porphyreon.

Then we came to—what do you think? The tomb of Jonah! The Moslems have built a mausoleum there. It is white, and has a dome on the top of it. It contains rooms for the keeper, and to accommodate pilgrims. Whether the Moslems really believe that Jonah is buried there I know not, but they do believe that it is the spot where the fish cast him ashore. They call the place "Neby Yunas," which is Arabic for "Prophet Jonah."

After a little time we crossed another river, the Oweley. This we crossed on a bridge. It is a narrow river. Soon afterward the sight of old Sidon gladdened my eyes, for the ride had been tedious, though I had seen a great many things which interested me. The road was terrible, all the time over rocks or through deep sand. If you look at the map you will see that the road lies close by the sea-shore, and we had the Mediterranean for a companion all day long. It is a calm, gentle sea, with small waves rolling constantly on the beach. This sea is almost tideless—the tide never rising higher than ten inches.

The city of Sidon, which Joshua calls *great*, and which was once renowned far and near, is now quite small. There is very little in the city itself which is interesting. There are but few ruins. There are six khans. We are staying at the best one, but it is full of discomfort. We intend to avoid khans as much as possible in our journeys; we all prefer "camping out."

There are a great many mulberry orchards in the neighborhood, the leaves of which are used for food for the silk-worm. Silk and tobacco are the chief exports of the place.

They have most delicious fruits here. I have as many oranges and bananas as I want, and drink scarcely anything but lemonade. The orange and lemon groves are beautiful; buds, and flowers, and fruit all hang on the same trees at the same time, and the air is constantly filled with the most delicious fragrance.

There are several cemeteries in Sidon. Each sect has its own. Every time I have visited one I have seen women mourning over the graves. They shriek and scream; they throw themselves on the ground; they tear their clothes and their hair. These women are *hired* by the real mourners, and "do up" so much grief for so much money. The funerals here seem to be conducted somewhat in the style of an Irish wake. A great feast is given, and all the friends invited have a jolly time. In olden times they had a very queer fashion of collecting the tears of mourners, and putting them in bottles and placing them in the tomb. These bottles were called lachrymatories.

They have been found in great numbers in the old tombs opened in this country. I have had two given to me—the first of my stock of curiosities. Mine are made of glass; they have a funnel-shaped top, long neck and broad bottom.

The hills around here are said to be full of old sepulchres—most of them caves cut out of solid rock.

I have seen very few ladies since I have been here, and they are all closely veiled. If you visit at any house, except those of the Franks, you will see no women; nothing but men. The women are kept shut up in the harem. I think they must have a terribly stupid time of it—don't you? They dress very much like men here, except the long veils and head-dresses. Some of these last are beautiful. I saw one yesterday that your sister would be glad to have. It was a pretty little red cap, with golden tassels; the cap was nearly covered with small glittering jewels. I was not able to get a glimpse of the face of the wearer of this, though I looked long and anxiously, for I thought nobody that was not young and pretty would wear such a cap as that.

These people have very queer ways. We went to a dinner-party a day or two ago in the house of a native. When we entered the room we found all the company seated cross-legged on their cushions, very gravely smoking their pipes. These pipes were various in fashion. Some of them were very beautiful, with long flexible tubes, and cut-glass bottles to hold the water, for they prefer their smoke to pass through water before inhaling it. They all rose up as we entered, making the most solemn bows, or salaams as they would say. Coffee was passed around soon after our arrival. I managed to drink mine, as there was not much of it. It was served in tiny cups of china and silver, very pretty.

The Arabs keep on their turbans all the time, and always slip off their shoes before entering the room. This is because they always sit on cushions with their feet doubled up under them. We took off our hats, kept on our shoes, and sat on divans which had been provided expressly for our use.

The silence and gravity soon disappeared. A few of the company understood English, but most of them talked in Arabic, in very loud tones, and faster than I ever imagined people could talk. I could often tell what they were saying from their expressive gestures. Father and Mr. Hamilton are Arabic scholars, and Hartley and I talked to the few who could muster a little English.

In a couple of hours servants came in bringing little round tables. On each of these was placed a tray with dishes containing the food. Four or five gathered around each table and fell to eating. We had no plates, or knives and forks. The dishes were all stews, or soups, or sauces. Pieces of bread were placed before each one. This Arab bread is made in the thinnest possible cakes, and is tolerably good. The Arabs eat with this bread by doubling it up, spoon fashion, and dipping it into the dishes. We foreigners were furnished with wooden spoons, and, though you may be surprised at my want of nicety, I dipped my spoon into the dishes pretty often, for these soups and stews are delicious, if all do eat out of the same dish. All drink out of the same water-pitcher also, but we were furnished with glasses, out of respect for our Western habits I suppose.

After the tables were taken away servants went around with a pitcher and basin. You hold your hands over the basin while the servant pours water on them and gives you the napkin to dry them with. This answers the purpose better than the finger bowls we use.

If I was not vastly entertained with the conversation, I was with the curious customs, and was glad I had attended this remarkable dinner-party.

The gardens of this city are beautiful. In the summer they must be magnificent. Now they are green with foliage, but only a few fruits and flowers are in season.

The streets, like those of Beirut, are narrow, crooked and dirty, and I have seen in them pretty much the same sights I saw there. One curious thing I have noticed about the houses here. The walls are covered with maxims, or quotations from the poets; or sentences from the Koran in Moslem houses, and from the Bible in Christian houses. I spoke to father about it, and he said that Moses commanded the children of Israel to write the precepts of the Lord upon their door-posts and gates. I think this must have been because they had no books.

This morning I saw a funeral procession, but it was not very solemn. The women went first by themselves, throwing their arms about and shrieking like wild creatures. The men and boys were crowded together in a grand mass, and were singing, "Ya Allah! Ya Allah!" (which is Arabic for O God! O God!) "La Allah illa Allah!" (no God but God!) and "Muhammedhn russul Allah!" (and Mohammed is the prophet of God). After a time they stopped and formed a ring, when two men in the centre of the circle began to jump about like wild cats, twisting their heads and jerking their bodies, until one of them tumbled down, and then they all thought he was in a divine trance, though I suspect he had a hysteric fit, which is not to be wondered at considering the performance he had just gone through with. Then they all took up the line of march again and soon disappeared.

While I am talking about the curious customs I will tell you about the Douseh. This is a religious ceremony given in honor of the dervishes, who do a great many wonderful tricks on this occasion. They throw sharp instruments into their eyes and cheeks and draw them out without hurting themselves. Whether they really throw them in, or only appear to, I can't say. Then a long *pavement of boys* is formed. The boys lay flat down, with their faces to the ground—one with his head to the south, the next with his feet to the south, and so on, alternating head and feet. The dervishes ride their horses over this living pavement, and it is said the boys are unhurt by this proceeding. Whether they are unhurt, or not, it is a very slavish and a very disgusting ceremony, I think. This is only done on extraordinary occasions, and it is not probable I shall ever witness it, but a gentleman who lives here has twice seen it, and he told me about it.

I hope I shall have a chance to see some

whirling dervishes. If I don't meet with them in this country we will find them in Constantinople, if we return that way. You have heard of them. Their form of worship is whirling about. They say they are inspired by God to do this, and they keep whirling until the inspiration passes off. Those who have seen them say the performance is slow and rather graceful at first, but they whirl faster and faster until they get quite frantic; their faces have a "rapt" expression, and their minds seem entirely withdrawn from earthly things. This may be because of the muddled condition their brains must be in after such a spinning round. The whole thing reminds one of that play the girls have that they call "making cheeses."

To-morrow we are going up the mountain to visit the place where Lady Hester Stanhope lived so many years.

Your affectionate friend,

PHILIP.

IV.

SIDON, Dec. 5, 18—.

MY DEAR HARRY:—

I should not have written to you from Sidon again, had I not promised to give you an account of our visit to the house which formerly belonged to Lady Hester Stanhope.

Quite a large party had been made up to go with us—all Franks—most of them English. Among them were four ladies. We rode out of the gate of Sidon at sunrise, but, early as it was, there were a great many loungers there, and I flattered myself we made quite a distinguished appearance as we cantered over the plain. Hartley and I had seen so many different styles of dress since we came to this country that we were tired of our commonplace American style, and concluded we would "flourish out" on this occasion. So we each wore an aba, which is a cloak worn by all classes of Arabs, made of various materials. Our's were quite short; they were made of dark brown silk, ornamented with gold and silver thread, and were what Caroline would call "very dashy." We wore red caps trimmed with gold cord. Father thought we bought these as curiosities to take home with us, and was quite surprised when we made our appearance with our red caps, and gold trimmings sparkling in the sunlight. The whole party laughed at our Oriental appearance, which was all the compliment we received, and I can't say that we found the change in our attire altogether comfortable; but we knew we looked well, which is a great matter.

We rode at a brisk pace, and were not long in reaching the Oweley. If you look at the map you will see that the little village of Joon is but a short distance from the river. It is situated on a mountain side, and on the very top of the mountain is Dahr Joon, where the Lady Hester lived.

Riding over the high hills and up the mountain side would have been very grand, if it had not been so very frightful. I don't think, Harry, that I am a very great coward, and I confess that I turned pale more than once as my little pony walked gingerly along the edge of a precipice, or down a steep and rocky path into a deep ravine. Father looked a little anxious about me, but was quite relieved when he saw how very cautious I was. He told me I must accustom myself to face such dangers if

I would become a traveller, and that when I travelled over the Lebanon mountains I would meet with worse roads than that which leads to Dahr Joon. By that time I shall have become accustomed to bad roads, but I never rode close to the edge of precipices until that day. The ladies, I noticed, were quite fearless—they are used to these barbarous roads. My little Saladin was very sure-footed, and trod along these narrow rocky paths as if he had been used to them all his days, as it is very probable that he has been.

The road was desolate and solitary, generally winding over barren hills or down into narrow stony valleys. These valleys are here called wadies. A few goats were wandering about, attended by their keepers, and occasionally we would come across a little cluster of Arab tents. Once I caught sight of a village in the distance, with olive orchards near it. I was surprised at this sight and pointed it out to a lady, and she told me that there were villages, cornfields and orchards in plenty among these stony valleys and barren-looking mountains.

Once, on making a sudden turn in the road, we came upon a very queer sight. It was so unexpected, and I was so unprepared for it, having never heard of such a thing, that I burst out laughing. Hartley joined me, which was very impolite of us, as the objects we were laughing at were ladies. They were mounted on mules, and looked like a company of ghosts with their long white dresses and thick veils. And, to give them a still more unearthly appearance, each one had a long horn growing out of her head? That is, they seemed to grow out of their heads, but they were really made of silver, and fastened on to the head somehow. Over these they hang their veils. These horns were about two feet long, and you may imagine the effect. These were grand ladies—they were Druse ladies of very high rank—ladies of lower rank wear smaller horns. I think these women must have very empty heads or they never could bear the weight of such horns.

The road grew worse as we went up the mountain, and at last we dismounted from our horses and climbed up a steep narrow path for two hundred feet. The house stands at the very top of the mountain. It looks like a great castle, with turrets and towers, and a high wall all around it. Nobody lives in it, and it is falling into ruin. The gardens, which were once very splendid, are filled with weeds and rubbish. The tomb is in the garden. We found our way to it with some difficulty. The vault was broken, and the arbor which had covered it was lying upon the ground. It was a picture of desolation. There was no inscription on the tomb. Not a living creature besides ourselves was to be seen. We could see the village of Joon on the side of a little mountain, just across the wady. I must say, I don't admire Lady Hester's taste in the selection of a place for her residence, especially as there are so many pretty places near. Perhaps she thought it very fine to look around her and see nothing but mountains on every side. Joon is steep and rocky, but I suppose she felt safer for that reason. But there is no water here, and all she used had to be brought up the mountain on mules.

Our luncheon was brought up in the same way; and, having found a clean shady place, we had our dinner of bread, chicken, figs, bananas and oranges, with lemonade for a beverage; and we enjoyed it, too, for we were famously hungry. As the day was warm, and it was quite pleasant on the mountain top, we concluded to wait a couple of hours before starting for Sidon. Some of the party wandered about the ruins, others lay down under the trees and went to sleep.

Mrs. Wilson, an English lady, had promised to tell the story of Lady Hester Stanhope to

Hartley and myself, for neither of us had ever heard it. So we fixed a seat under a terebinth tree and put cushions there for her, while we threw our cushions on the ground at her feet, and, having established ourselves comfortably, she told us the story. I had pencil and paper to take down the story for your benefit, but she has since kindly written it out for me. Here it is:—

"It would be almost impossible for me to give you a complete history of the life of this strange woman who ended her days up here in this lonely mountain of Dahr Joon, so varied and wonderful were her adventures. She was born in England, and was the grand-daughter of the Earl of Chatham and niece of William Pitt. She was a girl of rare abilities, and as soon as she was old enough Pitt chose her for his private secretary. She is described as being, at that time, very beautiful, witty and talented, and excessively romantic. She loved Sir John Moore. Of course you are familiar with the story of his life and his heroic death. The memory of this early love remained with Lady Hester all her life, and she never married.

"After the death of Pitt she received a pension of six thousand dollars a year from the English government. This income was certainly too small to enable her to move in the society to which she had been accustomed, in the style which she felt she ought to maintain. She regarded it as a mere pittance, and never forgave the English government for what she termed its ingratitude to the statesman who had done so much for his country. She determined to leave Europe and come to the East, partly because of the simple mode of life here, but chiefly, I expect, because she hoped that here she might find opportunities for gratifying her ambition, which would be impossible in Europe. To acquire absolute power had been the dream of her childhood and youth; and, from the time she left England, it was the goal towards which all her efforts were directed.

"After she came here she could never be persuaded to return to England. She knew every language of Europe and Asia, and could converse with the wild Arabs of the desert as easily as she could with the princes and distinguished men of every nation who visited her. After a time she gained great ascendancy over the Arab tribes, and they delighted in nothing so much as doing her bidding. They made her Queen of Palmyra, and she ruled them right royally. She used to wear the dress of an Emir—weapons, pipe and all. She was a splendid horsewoman, and rode at the head of her guard of mourted Albanian soldiers, whom she always kept about her. She had spies at the different cities, and at the courts of Pachas and Emirs, and knew everything that was going on in the countries around, which knowledge she turned to her own account.

"After leading a wandering and romantic life for some years she rented a lonely house, which was situated on the mountain of Joon, added many rooms to it, built a wall around it, fortified it strongly, and called it Dahr Joon. Dahr means hall or court, and here, for many years, she held her court. And now, having given up the comforts of her English home· having separated herself forever from her relatives and friends; having hardened her heart until it was without sympathy for her kind; disdaining the refinements of civilized life; scoffing at the religion of Christ; she had gained in return for all these the object of her ambition—the desire of her life. She did indeed possess absolute power, and woe to that man in Syria, be he prince or slave, who dared to interfere with or to dispute her authority. And who were her subjects? Her own Arab servants and negro slaves; the wretched and degraded inhabitants of the neighboring villages; and, for a time, those lawless robbers, the Bedouin Arabs. She had more influence, too, than any woman, probably, in modern times. And whom did she influence? Ignorant Pachas and vulgar Emirs; mixing herself up with their petty squabbles and disgraceful intrigues. I think her own soul must have been filled with disgust at herself; and no doubt it was. We have the testimony of one who knew her intimately at this time, that there was not a more wretched woman on the face of the earth.

"And what did the wild Arabs and uncivilized inhabitants of Syria gain from their intercourse with the most talented and influential woman of her age? Nothing. What a commentary on years of absolute power, that, when it was all over, and the restless spirit, which had ruled so long, was at rest forever, the people she had governed were as ignorant, degraded, and brutalized, as when she first appeared among them. If she had used her talents and influence to elevate, civilize, and Christianize the natives of Syria, what a vast amount of good she might have accomplished! No woman ever had such opportunities before. No one could more utterly have wasted and abused them. No wonder that she was unhappy. No wonder that her temper grew more and more violent, and that her fits of passion were terrible. She did not even make one friend among the natives. They all deceived her; stole from her; and, in her poverty, left her to die.

"Her income was not sufficient to meet her expenses, and every year she got deeper and deeper into debt, until, at last, she was utterly ruined. She was now old, and her charms of person and manner were gone. She was in feeble health, and no longer able to terrify with her lightning glance and terrible tongue. And then her power and influence melted away like a thin vapor, and she was left to reflect how unsubstantial it all had been. Her guards gradually deserted her. Her servants neglected her when she was sick, and robbed her. She could hear them breaking open chests, and ripping up cushions, when she was too ill to prevent them. She dismissed them, but those who took their places were no better. Poor Lady Hester! We do not know what were her thoughts in those awful days, for she had no one to whom to confide them. The few Europeans who had followed her to Syria, and remained faithful to her for many years, were dead, or had been compelled to leave her long before, and she died at the age of seventy-three, without a European attendant, and without a friend.

"Her funeral ceremonies were performed by an American missionary of Sidon; two English-

6

men were with him. It was found necessary to inter the body soon after their arrival at Joon, and she was buried at midnight. A French general had been put into this vault years before, and the servants had gathered his bones up in a heap near the entrance, with the skull on the top. Candles were stuck in the eye-sockets, and by the light of these Lady Hester's body was committed to the ground.

"It was rather a curious coincidence, that she should have been buried in this manner—so similar, in many respects, to the burial of her early lover, Sir John Moore, very many years before. You remember the account how he was buried hastily, at midnight, in a lonely spot on the battle-field, by a few attendants, for the enemy was advancing on them:—

"'We buried him darkly, at dead of night,
The sods with our bayonets turning;
By the struggling moonbeams' misty light,
And the lantern dimly burning.'

"As for the treasures she had collected during her long life, none were found in the house after her death. Her rooms were examined by the English Consul of Sidon, and found to be filled with rubbish. One was piled up with old, worm-eaten saddles, all that was left of her Albanian guard. Another was full of pipe-stems. Some were filled with physic, for she pretended to a great knowledge of medicine among other things. There were plenty of books, although she was never a great reader. But everything valuable had been stolen by her attendants. A very wealthy man in Sidon is said to have made his fortune in this way.

"The life of Lady Hester would be incomplete if I did not say something about the means she took to establish her influence over all around her. Her lavish expenditure of money was, no doubt, part of the secret, but, after all, the real power lay in herself. She had the art of charming her equals, so that they felt a pleasure in submitting to her will, and her inferiors she terrified into obedience. And then she had such great penetration. Her power of finding out the inmost secrets of the human heart seemed absolutely miraculous, and made her greatly feared. She could do generous acts, too, in a princely way. The reason she built so large a house was, that, in the numerous wars which were always breaking out in Syria, the poor, and oppressed, and houseless might come to her, and find a home. And she welcomed all who came to her for protection, even those she was known to hate, and neither flatteries, threats, or violence would make her give them up. But then they, as well as all others who approached her, must do as she bid them.

"She had great physical and moral courage. She has faced those sent to kill her with a boldness that has frightened them from their purpose, and I think we may safely say she never knew fear. In her arbitrary way she was also very kind to the poor and sick.

"On the whole, it was a strange life she led up here in Dahr Joon—now riding at the head of wild Arabs, as Queen of the Desert; now scolding the gardener about his lettuce beds; now dictating a letter of political advice to a Prince; the next moment telling her maid how to cut out her apron; at one time treating with contempt consuls, generals, and nobles, and ordering officers sent to her lodge to be whipped, and, directly after, resorting to the meanest shifts to avoid her creditors; one day kind and charitable to the poor, the next treating them with cruelty and harshness.

"I think she may be said to have had no religious faith, as she thought all systems of religion nearly equally good. She either believed, or pretended to believe, that the Messiah was yet to come, and she was to act a very important part at that time. She and the

Messiah were to ride into Jerusalem side by side. She kept two beautiful mares, named Laila and Luda, which were never suffered to be ridden, as these were for the use of the Messiah and herself. One of these had a singularly-shaped back. Its backbone sank suddenly down at the shoulders, and rose abruptly near the hips. This deformity she imagined to be a miraculous saddle, on which she was to ride into Jerusalem. Both these animals were attended with great care. They had comfortable rooms, in which lamps were kept constantly burning. They were fed with sherbet and other delicacies. After Lady Hester's death, these poor, pampered creatures were sold to farmers in the neighborhood, and hard work and poor fare soon put an end to their miserable lives.'

We were very much interested in this account of Lady Hester, and begged Mrs. Wilson to tell us something more about her; but she said she would tell us a short story instead—one that was written by St. Jerome, whose cell we would see at the convent at Bethlehem. She said the two stories should be related together, because they were both about persons who did nothing for mankind or the good of the world, and lived to old age, solely intent on their own advancement—the one desiring to be great on earth, the other to be great in heaven.

"A certain holy anchorite had passed a long life in a cave, remote from all communion with men, and he fasted, and prayed, and performed many severe penances, and his whole thought was how he should make himself of account in the sight of God, that he might enter into his Paradise.

"After having lived this life for threescore and ten years, he was puffed up with the notion of his own great virtue and sanctity, and, like to St. Anthony, he besought the Lord to show him what saint he should emulate as greater than himself; thinking, perhaps, in his heart that the Lord would answer that none was greater or holier. And the same night the Angel of God appeared to him, and said:—'If thou wouldst excel all others in virtue and sanctity, thou must strive to be like a certain minstrel, who goes begging and singing from door to door.'

"And the holy man was in great astonishment, and he arose and took his staff, and ran forth in search of the minstrel; and, when he had found him, he questioned him earnestly, saying, 'Tell me, I pray thee, my brother, what good works thou hast performed in thy lifetime, and by what prayers and penances thou hast made thyself acceptable to God?'

"And the man, greatly wondering, and ashamed to be so questioned, hung down his head, as he replied, 'I beseech thee, holy father, mock me not! I have performed no good works, and as for praying, alas! sinner that I am, I am not worthy to pray, except to ask God to forgive my wickedness. I do nothing but go about from door to door, amusing the people with my viol and my flute.'

"But the holy man insisted, and said, 'Nay, but peradventure, in the midst of this, thy evil life, thou hast done some good works?' The minstrel replied, 'I know of nothing good that I have done.' The hermit, wondering more and more, said, 'How hast thou become a beggar? Hast thou spent thy substance in riotous living, like most others of thy calling?'

"And the man, answering, said, 'Nay; but there was a poor woman, whom I found running hither and thither in distraction, for her husband and children had been sold into slavery, to pay a debt. So I took her home to my hut, and protected her, and I gave her all I had to redeem her family, and conducted her in safety to the city, where she was re-united to her husband and children. But what of that, my father? Is there a man who would not have done the same?'

"And the hermit, hearing these words, wept bitterly, saying, 'For my part, I have not done so much good in all my life, and they call me a man of God, and thou art only a poor minstrel?'"

And then Mrs. Wilson recited a poem, which is on the same subject. It was written by an Englishman, and is prettier even, I think, than the story of St. Jerome. I have since learned it, and will write it down for you and Caroline to learn:—

"Abou Ben Adhem (may his tribe increase)
Awoke one night from a sweet dream of peace,
And saw, within the moonlight in his room,
Making it rich, and like a lily in bloom,
An Angel writing in a book of gold.
Exceeding peace had made Ben Adhem bold;
And to the Presence in the room he said,
'What writest thou?'. The Vision raised its head,
And, with a look made of all sweet accord,
Answered, 'The names of those who love the Lord.'
'And is mine one?' said Abou. 'Nay, not so,'
Replied the Angel. Abou spake more low,
But cheerily still, and said, 'I pray you then,
Write me for one who loves his fellow-men.'
The Angel wrote, and vanished. The next night
He came again, with great, awakening light,
And showed the names whom love of God had blest,
And lo! Ben Adhem's name led all the rest!"

At four o'clock we left Dahr Joon to its loneliness, and rode slowly over the breakneck roads back to old Sidon. On our return over the plain, we stopped to look at some men who were ploughing. It was a curious sight. No less than six ploughs were following each other in the same furrow! Each plough has a yoke of oxen and a driver. The ploughs were wretched little things. I could have lifted one with the greatest ease. And the oxen were not larger than good-sized heifers are in our part of the world. The ploughs do not sink very deeply, but scratch up the ground at the top, which may be the reason that so many ploughs go over the same track. Lands cultivated this way are owned in common, or belong to Government. The ploughmen like this way of working, as it gives them a chance to gossip. But what a lazy way of doing things!

It is an old custom, though. Father asked me if I remembered the account of the calling of Elisha—he was ploughing with twelve yoke of oxen, and he with the twelfth. I remembered it well, for I had often puzzled my head over it. What he wanted with so many oxen, and how he could yoke himself with the twelfth! But now it was as clear as daylight to me. There were twelve ploughs and twelve yoke of oxen, and twelve drivers, all in a line.

He was with the twelfth yoke as a driver. I am constantly finding out that the reason some of the things told in the Bible seem impossible to me, is because of my own great ignorance.

We will leave Sidon and its pleasant and hospitable people to-morrow. Everybody, both Franks and natives, have been so kind to us since we have been here, that I shall be sorry to leave them.

Your affectionate friend,

PHILIP.

V.

TYRE, Dec. 10, 18—.

MY DEAR HARRY:—

You will naturally expect my account of this place to be particularly interesting, but I fear you will be disappointed. I have not been very greatly entertained here, and a two days' storm has put me in such a state of stupidity that it will be wonderful if some of it does not get into my letter.

But, according to custom, I will first tell you about our journey from Sidon to this place. How familiar are the words, "the coast of Tyre and Sidon." They are frequently mentioned in Bible history, and certain it is, that our Saviour once travelled through all the region I have been wandering over, for the last few days. We left Sidon on the sixth, pitched our tents near Sarepta in the afternoon, and remained there all night, and the next morning resumed our journey to this city, which we reached at noon. The distance is generally calculated at eight hours, but we chose to take matters slowly, which makes travel much more enjoyable.

On the road from Sidon to Sarepta we saw several houses with white domes; occasionally a village with two or three of these in it. Mr. Hamilton tells me that these white-domed houses cover the shrines of prophets or holy men. Judging from the numbers we have seen during the short time we have been in the country, I should suppose that there had been a large collection of holy men in this region. Nearly every high hill has on it a sacred place —a willy or mazar, as they are called by the natives—and to these the people go to worship. Some of these are very old, so old that it is not known whether they were built by Jews, Christians, Mohammedans, or Arabs, and therefore all these sects claim them, and use them in different ways for the same purpose. Father says these are the "high places" so frequently condemned in the Old Testament. They are generally situated in a grove or under a single tree.

When we arrived at Sarepta, we found our tents pitched under some tamarisk trees. After dinner we lay down for some time under the trees, for the sun was pretty hot by this time. As I lay there I began to understand how it is that people who live here long get into such lazy habits. Everything around me was so quiet, and the air made me feel dreamy, not sleepy. I had a feeling that it would be much more agreeable to lie there always, and look up into the soft, clear Syrian sky, and think of all the splendid things I intended to do, than to have to work hard all my life, as we Western people do. And then, you know, one can think of things so much more splendid than he can ever do, let him work hard as he may. It was like a romance to me, any way, being there at all. I would shut my eyes for a few moments, then turn my head in any direction, and suddenly open them, always seeing something I was not accustomed to—palm trees, lovely little gazelles, queer-looking camels, and queerer-looking Arabs, the long wave of drifted sand, and the light feathery trees above me. I thought of Philadelphia, and how it was full of people, toiling from morning till night at all sorts of trades, manufactures and professions; heavily-loaded drays going through the streets; carts, wagons, and omnibuses rattling over the pavements; men, women, boys, girls, and horses all hard at work. Oh, dear! it fairly made me groan! And our old school-room rose before me. O! but there is plenty of hard work done there! I thought of you, Mr. Harry, poring over your books, and wishing yourself on the pond, skating. Skating! How that word changed the current of my ideas. I would not live in this country on any account, beautiful as it is. No snow! no skating! no sledding!

During these reflections everybody was asleep but me. When they woke up we four travellers started for a survey of Sarepta and the surrounding country. I should say Sarafend, for that is the name it is now known by, and I expect that is the only name you will find on your map. But I like the old names best. The ruins of Sarepta extend for a mile along the shore, and they are really ruins; there is very little shape or form about them. They have been dug over a great many times for building stones. Workmen were digging out stones when we were there. We asked them what they were going to do with them? They told us they were going to take them to Beirut! These people have no reverence and respect for ancient things. They would tumble down the wall of a splendid temple, which had stood for centuries, with no more emotion than we would feel in overturning an old shed. No wonder that all traces of the very ancient cities of this country are entirely lost. In the neighborhood of Sarepta there is quite a large extent of country which is covered with rubbish, which rubbish was once ruins, which ruins marked the site of an ancient Greek city, called Ornithon. Thousands of years ago Ornithon disappeared from the face of the earth; hundreds of years ago Sarepta passed away, and now the little village of Sarafend is all that is left of them.

Sarepta is called Zarephath in the Old Testament. It was here the widow lived who entertained Elijah, and gave him of the little food she had when there was a famine. For this act of kindness, the Lord did not suffer her barrel of meal to waste, or cruse of oil to fail during the famine.* In Sarafend they showed us the cave where the widow had lived—at least so they told us.

The next morning we continued our journey, riding near the blue waves of the Mediterranean, and sometimes *in* them. We saw no villages, which I thought strange, but Mr. Hamilton says the people who cultivate these plains live among the mountains, and come down to the plain to do their work. This is because they are afraid of the wandering Arabs. When the Phœnicians lived here the whole coast was covered with great cities and thriving villages. That is because they were

* 1 Kings xvii.

seamen, and it was convenient for them to live on the sea-coast. I don't believe the present inhabitants know how to manage boats; I have not seen a boat on the sea during our journey.

If you will examine your map, you will see that before we reached Tyre we had to cross a river, called Kasimieh. Tracing the river up from its mouth, you will find it is a very long river, and that higher up it is called the Litany. It is the largest river, except the Orontes, which empties into this part of the Mediterranean. It is said to be a very beautiful river where it winds among the mountains, and some of these days we will pay it a visit. On the banks of this river I counted twenty young gazelles, drinking. At our approach they bounded gracefully away over the plain.

Near the city we saw a fountain, called Babuk, and around it are the ruins of an ancient city. There we had a fine view of Mount Hermon, which the Arabs call Jibel-es-Sheikh (Mountain of the Chief), not a bad name for the grand old fellow, which lifts its head so high above all others, and puts a stop to the long range of Lebanon mountains.

As for Tyre itself, it is the most meagre collection of insignificant villages, with no walls, no public works, not even ruins of any interest (if we except the cathedral), and an empty harbor. Intelligent Europeans, who live in this country, tell us that there *are* magnificent ruins all around us, or rather *underneath* us, for they say that great temples and palaces are buried in the ground, with heaps of stones and rubbish piled on them, which have been accumulating for hundreds of hundreds of years. Persons have built houses on top of these temples, and lived there for a lifetime, never dreaming what splendor was beneath them. When I get to be a man I intend to excavate some of these old cities, if somebody don't do it before me. Parts of the ancient wall of Tyre lie buried under the sand heaps, and can be seen by those who choose to go to the trouble and expense of having the sand thrown off them.

The day we arrived here we were rowed round the city in a boat. It was the first time I had been on the Mediterranean in an open boat. We were shown a large stone let in the old wall of Tyre, which is just as as it was when first placed there, thousands of years ago. It is seventeen feet long—a pretty good-sized stone. It is close down by the water. By looking down to the bottom of the sea, we could see great numbers of granite columns, some of them very large. They once belonged to buildings which have been thrown into the sea by earthquakes, or the sea changing its bed, or something of the kind. I wonder the people here don't try to raise them, as they are so anxious for building materials. I have some beautiful specimens of marble, of various colors, which I broke off fragments of columns near the sea.

Once upon a time, there was in Tyre a great cathedral, over two hundred feet long, and eighty feet high. Hartley says it was built in the morning twilight of Christianity, which is his poetical way of saying that no one knew when or by whom it was built. In it was laid the body of Origen, one of the earliest Christian writers, and in it was buried the Emperor Frederic Barbarossa. At this present time it is a complete wreck; scarcely any part of it is left standing. The great area is filled up with mean hovels, in which dwell a dirty race of peasants. This is all I can tell you of the most interesting ruin which Tyre possesses.

We only expected to remain here two days, but on the afternoon of the second day there commenced such a storm, the like of which you never saw, I think—I mean in amount of rain. It poured down almost incessantly for two days, and it seemed to me there was one continuous sheet of water descending perpetually from the sky to the earth. Yesterday the rain was a little less violent, but the wind blew nearly a hurricane. The sea, which has been so constantly calm and blue, looked then like black broth boiling in a kettle. Of course nobody could think of going out of doors, and we amused ourselves the best we could in the house. Hartley and I spent a good deal of time watching the sea, which is only a few yards from the khan. Occasionally we took a game of chess, but oftener coaxed Ibrahim to tell us stories. He has a very entertaining way of relating stories, and his broken English makes them amusing, but when I undertake to write them down I find they are really very silly things. They are pretty much in the style of the Arabian Nights, only not half so good; all about genii and evil demons;—King Solomon plays a conspicuous part in most of them.

This morning Ibrahim called us early to go to the sea-shore with him. The morning was bright and beautiful; the sky without a cloud, the sea as calm and blue as if it had never been disturbed by wind or rain. The beach was covered with shells, most of them new to me. There were thousands of what I took to be small conch shells. They were like them in shape, but I found they were much thinner than conch shells, almost transparent in fact, and so brittle that I could easily crush them in my hand. They were beautifully colored. Ibrahim told us that in old times people who lived in Tyre, in the days when it was a great and powerful city, used these shells to dye beautiful purple and crimson cloths, which were sent to all parts of the world, and much sought after by kings and queens, being very rich and very costly. I had read a great deal about the famous Tyrian purple, and looked at these shells with curiosity. I asked Ibrahim if this was the only place where they could be found. He said they were scattered all along the coast—there were more of them about the bay of Acre than anywhere else—after a storm they could be gathered by loads; but they were so delicate the waves washing over them soon broke them to pieces. I asked him how they got the coloring out of the shells. He said they broke them up in mills and other ways, and that seemed to be all he knew about it. I asked him why no one tried now-a-days to make this beautiful dye—"you, for instance, Ibrahim," said I, thinking I would stir up some ambition in him; "why don't you set up a dyeing establishment and find out how to color those beautiful cloths? You are a smart man, and there is no reason why you shouldn't send your cloth over the whole world and have it worn by kings and queens; and soon, instead of being a courier, you will be a very rich and great man."

He listened respectfully, as he always does to everything we say, but when I finished he only said: "Young Amelican gentleman think poor Arab know everything—do everything; but poor Arab poor beast."

This opinion I had had for some time, but was too polite to tell Ibrahim so. Here they are in one of the most charming climates, which they care nothing for; with good soil, which they only half cultivate; with a sea on which they have not a ship; with fine rivers, on whose waters is neither steamboat or sloop, and on whose banks are no factories; with grand old ruins which they tumbled down to get stones for their miserable hovels.

As soon as we returned to the khan I hastened to show father my treasures, which he was very glad to see. I told him, also, of the fine prospects I had held out to Ibrahim, but he seemed to think Ibrahim would not succeed with his dyeing establishment, even if he had the energy and knowledge necessary; for the Tyrian purple, which was so celebrated in ancient times, would probably be worth little now, as we have so many beautiful colors and fine cloths, such as the old Tyrians never dreamed of. I thought all this very likely, and I told

Ibrahim after breakfast that he might as well give up the dyeing establishment, but I had nc doubt I should find some business equally as good for him before I left the country. I have some shells carefully put away for you, but I doubt whether I shall be able to take them safely to America.

When the storm commenced we had just returned from a visit to Ras-el-Ain, which means "fountain head." Here there are several large fountains, or "springs," as we generally call them in America. The waters of some of these have been collected into four large reservoirs, fifteen or twenty feet high. These four were in ancient times connected together by small aqueducts, and the water was carried through great aqueducts to Tyre. The distance is about four miles. We rode by the aqueduct most of the way. It is in ruins, although the water is still carried by it for a couple of miles to El Mushuk, where it is used for turning mills. This aqueduct is very old, having been built, probably, by the Romans. But the reservoirs, or "birkehs," as they are called here, are much older—so old that no tradition tells when they were built. They are thought to have been here during the reign of Solomon, when, you will recollect, Hiram was king of

Tyre. As old as Solomon! Only think of it! There are broad walks around the tops of the walls of these reservoirs; and, as I walked around the largest one I thought perhaps Solomon and his friend Hiram had walked in the very spot where my footsteps were treading. Who knows?

Hiram's tomb is not very far from the fountains, and we visited it. It is an ugly, massive-looking monument, built of five immense stones, laid one above another, of which the third stone is the largest and the fifth the smallest. The height of the monument is twenty feet. The stones are very grey and weather-beaten, and we all agreed it looked old enough to be the tomb of Hiram. Tradition says it was built for him; but we have no means of knowing certainly. I choose to think it was his, and that he once lay in the sarcophagus which was to be seen on the top of it a few years ago.

We took our lunch under some fig trees near by; and then, as we saw the angry clouds gathering in the sky, we took to our horses and scampered off to Tyre. As we drew near the village father pointed out to me some fishermen drying their nets in the rocks, now bare, which were once covered with the temples of ancient Tyre, and repeated these words:—

"And they shall destroy the walls of Tyrus, and break down her towers; I will also scrape her dust from her, and make her like the top of a rock. It shall be a place for the spreading of nets in the midst of the sea: for I have spoken it, saith the Lord God; and it shall become a spoil to the nations."*

Father said I must give you some idea of what you may learn of Tyre in the Bible. We looked out all the places during the rainy days. The first mention of the city is in Joshua, where it is called "a strong city." It is mentioned as part of the land given to the tribe of Asher, although the Jews never actually owned any part of the sea-coast. In the second book of Samuel it tells how Hiram, king of Tyre, sent cedar-wood, carpenters and masons to David; also how Joel, in numbering the people, came to the "stronghold" of Tyre. In the first book of Kings, Solomon sends to Hiram "a cunning workman in brass," also gives him several cities. In Ezra cedar-wood was again obtained from Tyre for the rebuilding of the temple. In Nehemiah the Tyrians are mentioned as selling things to the Jews on the

* Exekiel xxvi. 3, 4, 5.

Sabbath. The city is mentioned several times in the Psalms. In the twenty-seventh chapter of Ezekiel you may read an account of the commerce Tyre had with the nations around her. The prophets all foretold her downfall. While our Saviour was on earth the wickedness of Tyre must have been great; for, speaking of the sinfulness of the cities of Galilee, he says: "Wo unto thee, Chorasin! wo unto thee, Bethsaida! for if the mighty works which were done in you had been done in Tyre and Sidon, they would have repented long ago in sackcloth and ashes." In Acts the Tyrians are spoken of among those who worshipped Herod as a god, and there was also a Christian church in that city, which was visited by Paul just before his departure for Rome.

Tyre was founded by a colony from Sidon, two hundred and forty years before the building of Solomon's temple. It was a very strongly-built city. The walls were almost impregnable. Seven hundred years before Christ the king of Assyria blockaded it for five years in vain. Nebuchednezzar laid siege to it for thirteen years, and history does not say whether he captured it then. Alexander took it after a siege of seven months. Afterwards the Romans had it in possession. Then the Moslems. The Crusaders dared not attack it until after they had been in the Holy City for twenty-five years. They then took it after a five months' siege. The Christians held it for one hundred and fifty years, when it again fell into the hands of the Moslems, who destroyed some of the fortifications. From that time it has dwindled down, until now it is but a paltry village. Several attempts have been made to rebuild it, but all have failed. The modern name of it is Sur.

Father has received a letter from Mr. Elliott, a very dear friend of his, who lives in New England. He is now in Jerusalem, and expects soon to leave the country, as he has travelled all over it. He wishes father to spend Christmas with him in Jerusalem. This alters our plans a little, though we had intended to be in Bethlehem on Christmas day. Now we shall go directly from here to Jerusalem.

Your affectionate

VI.

JERUSALEM, Dec. 20, 18—.

MY DEAR HARRY:—

The Holy City of the Holy Land! It is my home now, and has been for six days. Our journey from Tyre was rather wearisome, and we met with no accident. On our arrival here we found Mr. Elliott expecting us. He was visiting an English family whom he had known before he met them here. They kindly invited our party to spend our time with them, and pressed us so we found it impossible to refuse. The family consists of Mr. and Mrs. Fanshawe, two sons and a daughter, all grown up, and a lady, Miss Erskine, Mrs. Fanshawe's sister. It is much more agreeable to be here than at a hotel—that I know. They have rented a house and intend to stay here a year. Making this their home they will go to visit all the places they care to see. A very nice plan, isn't it? They have a very large and handsome house. The halls are laid with marble floors. The garden is quite large, and laid out very prettily. I enjoy it very much. Everything is so *comfortable*, just like home.

We have paid off and dismissed all our attendants except Ibrahim, so we will have to get another supply when we leave.

There are so many things to tell you about Jerusalem that I don't know where to begin. Father suggests that I first give you some idea of the general appearance of the city.

The modern city, like the ancient, is entirely enclosed within the walls, but the ancient walls extended much beyond the present. The city now is small in size, being only a mile long and half a mile broad. The population is small—the regular population I mean. There is always a great crowd of strangers here. During Lent and Easter the city is said to be fairly packed with visitors and pilgrims. It is the holiest of the holy cities of the Jews; the Moslems regard it as next to Mecca in their sacred places; they call it El Kuds (the holy); the Greek and Roman Catholics make pilgrimages to it, and even Protestants look forward to a visit to Jerusalem as the most desirable of journeys. It is certainly held in greater esteem than any other place on earth.

The city is divided into four distinct quarters, the Christian, Armenian, Jewish and Mahommedan.

The walls are high, never less than twenty-five feet, sometimes as high as forty. At short distances there are square towers, and there are many loop-holes in the walls. There is a path around the top protected by a breastwork, which makes a very fine promenade. Flights of steps, at convenient distances, lead up to this walk. There are four gates. On the west the gate is called Bethlehem, or Jaffa gate, because the road from it leads to those places. The Arabs call it Hebron gate. That on the north is called Damascus gate by the Franks—Gate of the Pillar by the Arabs. On the east is St. Stephen's gate; or, according to the Arabic, Gate of the Tribes. On the south is Zion gate; or, as the natives choose to name it, Gate of the Prophet David. There are also three gates which have been walled up. Two of these are small—one of these the Franks call the Gate of Herod, the Arabs the Flowery; the other is the Gate of the Western Africans. The third gate is a very large one, the "Golden Gate" of the Franks, the "Eternal Gate" of the Arabs.

I have visited all these gates. They are mostly square towers. The Golden Gate, although walled up on the outside is open within the city, and is the handsomest of them all. It has pillars in it and beautiful carved work. The Arabs walled up this gate because of a prophecy that when the Christians take the city they will enter through that gate. I think they are foolish to suppose a few stones will defeat the prophecy—as if the Christian nations could not enter the city whenever and wherever they choose! All the gates of the city are closed during the night—they are also closed at the hours of prayer on Friday, on account of another prophecy, that if the city is ever captured by the Christians it will be at that time.

I will give you the names of a few of the principal streets, which are the only ones much visited by travellers:—

1. Street of David, which you will see goes from Jaffa gate to the

2. Street of the Temple, which leads to what was in ancient times the Temple Area, but is now the Mosque of Omar, as you will see on your map.

3. Street of the Patriarch, leading north from Street of David to Church of the Holy Sepulchre.

4. Via Dolorosa, which leads from Street of the Patriarch to St. Stephen's gate.

5. Street of St. Stephen, leading through the markets to the Damascus gate.

The Via Dolorosa, or "Path of Sorrow," is, according to tradition, the path our Saviour had to take in his wearisome journey to Calvary, carrying his cross.

The "show places" of Jerusalem, what we would call the "lions of the city," are the following:—

Church of the Holy Sepulchre, a very large building on Calvary, owned by several different sects.

The Mosque of Omar.

The Convents—Greek, Latin and Armenian.

Church of St. James, a ruined Syrian church.

Arch of the "Ecce Homo!"* also called the Arch of Pilate. This spans the Via Dolorosa.

Church of the Flagellations, built, according to tradition, on the spot where Christ was scourged by Pilot.

Church of St. Ann, reputed birth-place of the Virgin Mary.

Church of the Forerunner.

The Schools—Greek and Moslem.

Hospital and Dispensary of the London Mission.

The Synagogues.

The Khans. These pretend to be hotels. They have pretty good accommodations for animals—men are expected to be capable of taking care of themselves. Travellers have to furnish their own rooms and find their own provisions.

*"Behold the man!" See John xix. 5.

I am glad we are so fortunate as to be in a private family.

The Bazaars.

College for Blind Dervishes. The Muezzins, who stand on the minarets and cry the hours of prayer, instead of ringing bells, are commonly taken from this college. The reason given for this is that they cannot see what their neighbors are doing on the housetops, where Eastern people spend most of their time.

As to the valleys of Jerusalem, you are familiar with their names. One runs through the city from the Damascus gate to the Pool of Siloam. This is called the Valley of the Cheesemongers. Of course there is a ridge on each side of this valley; that on the east is Mount Moriah, where, you know, the Temple was built; on the west is Mount Zion. On the north and east of the city is the Valley of Jehosaphat. The brook Kedron runs through it. On the north this valley is often called the Valley of the Kedron. On the east of this valley is the Mount of Olives; on the southeast the Mount of Offence. On the south and west is the Valley of Kinnom. South of this is the Hill of Evil Counsel. At the foot of the Mount of Olives, nearly opposite St. Stephen's gate, you will find the Garden of Gethsemane.

As the place possessing the most interest of any in Jerusalem, we should, I suppose, have visited first the Church of the Holy Sepulchre; but then we did not do it. The first day after our arrival here the elder gentlemen were busy with their own affairs, and left us young ones to our own devices.

William Fanshawe, Hartley and I set forth in the early morning, and spent the whole day roaming about the city; looking at the buildings, going into some of the churches, talking to the beggars, buying things at the bazaars, just for the fun of hearing the merchants praise their wares and flatter us, and various other things which I have forgotten. I know we spent a very pleasant day, and had a great deal of sport. But the walking was rather wearisome—all the time up, up, up, or down, down, down! Verily this is a hilly city! The streets are like those of the other cities we have seen in this country—badly paved and narrow, without sidewalks, and with a deep channel in the middle to let the water run off. They are very crooked. Many of the houses are built of a beautiful-colored limestone—a rich cream color streaked with blood red. I like it, but it looks odd. Some of the streets are paved with large round stones of the same color. Everything looked so very old. The buildings and arches and recesses were time-stained, and many of them overgrown with vines.

As for the people, I believe every nation under the sun has its representative here; and, as they all wear their native costumes, your curiosity is on the stretch and your excitement kept up all the time. We would often stop somebody and ask a question. Sometimes we would get a stare, sometimes a bow and a smile, some would shake their heads to let us know they did not understand us, and others would answer in some strange jargon. Once we met an Englishman; but, as he told us that we would be taken by the Turkish soldiers and put to the torture, that he had been robbed and nearly murdered since he had been in the country, that Jerusalem was the most unhealthy city in the world and the plague had broken out in it, we did not consider his style of conversation agreeable and soon left him.

Among other places we visited the Armenian convent, which is, I believe, the largest in the city. William Fanshawe is slightly acquainted with the Patriarch, and on the strength of this acquaintance he took us there, and we were shown all over the building by a priest, who spoke English and made himself very agreeable. He had a very pleasant face and I liked him. We saw the portraits of all the former patriarchs, who, since their death, have been made into saints. I hope the memories they have left behind them are more beautiful than the pictures. We saw the doors of a chapel which were made of tortoise shell inlaid with mother-of-pearl. They were very pretty and curious and costly. The walls were of mosaic, representing terrible fights between saints and devils. I suppose it was all very fine. I am not a judge of such things, but I found it hard work to decide which were the saints and which were the devils. We gave the priest some money for the poor and he gave us his benediction, whereupon we parted mutually pleased.

After leaving the convent we bought something to eat in the bazaar, and then Hartley proposed we should visit the Mosque of Omar, as the grounds looked very inviting to rest in. William Fanshawe told him he would have to turn Mussulman before he could be admitted into those grounds. Hartley thought he would rather not. William then said he would take us to Pilate's house, from which we could have a good view of the building and grounds. It seemed to me a funny idea to go to Pilate's house, and, thinking he was joking, I asked him if it would not do as well to go to Caiaphas' palace, but he assured me this was the very house of Pontius Pilate; or, at least, people said so, and he knew nothing to the contrary. We found nothing very magnificent about the house, but it looked old enough to have belonged to Pilate. From the roof we had a fine prospect.

The mosque, as you well know, stands on the spot once occupied by the temple. Indeed, it is said that some of the stones in its foundations were parts of the great temple itself. I don't know about this, but certain it is, that the present building is very beautiful. The mosque has eight sides, and stands on a square marble platform. This platform is in the highest part of what used to be the temple area. From it the ground slopes on every side down to the walls, which surround the whole enclosure. On the south side of the enclosure there is also a handsome mosque, called El-Aksa. Between the two is a great marble basin, filled with water and surrounded by trees. It looked as if inviting us to a plunge. But those savage-looking black men, who were guarding the gates, would have said a word or two to us if we had attempted anything of that kind. None but "the faithful" are allowed to enter these sacred grounds. They are very beautiful, planted with acacias and olives, cypresses and palms. White-veiled women were flitting about, looking ghost-like among the trees; turbaned Turks, in their gay dresses, were pacing gravely about, according to their fashion, and all seemed to be enjoying themselves. Suddenly from one of the minarets of the mosque there rung out a clear, silvery voice, crying, "There is no God but God, and Mohammed is the prophet of God!" This was the muezzin's call to prayer. Instantly every one in the grounds threw himself into some one of their numerous attitudes of prayer. This is a pretty custom, I think, in Mohammedan countries. They have stated hours for prayer. They permit no bells in their churches, but have men, called muezzins, stationed at the different minarets, who call out the regular hours, in the manner mentioned above. Then every Mohammedan, it makes no difference where he may be—in the street, at his counter, on his horse, no matter what urgent business he may have on hand, drops on his knees, and says his prayers.

As the sun was setting we would now have departed, had it not been for the conversation of a young man who had come up to the roof some time after us, and who was telling his younger brother all about the mosque. He talked so well that we liked to listen. He saw how interested we were, and told us if we would draw nearer he would tell us the history of the temple. I thought of you, and asked him if he had any objections to my writing it down, much to William Fanshawe's surprise and Hartley's mortification. But the stranger only smiled, and said he liked to see young people eager for information, and that I was at liberty to write as much as I pleased. So here is the story just as he told it.

"In the days of King Solomon, when Jerusalem was in its greatest glory, when silver was nothing accounted of, it was so plentiful, and gold was brought hither in immense quantities from Ophir; when the Jews were at peace with all the world, and Hiram, King of Tyre, was the friend of Solomon; in those days Solomon built, upon a chosen spot on Mount Moriah, a magnificent temple, which he dedicated to the Most High. This temple was one of the wonders and glories of the world. Its walls of fragrant cedars, adorned with gold; its great golden cherubims, and candlesticks, and golden altars; its rich purple and scarlet hangings, and curiously carved tables, were the talk of all the nations around. And when it was finished, Solomon assembled all the great people of the land, and solemnly dedicated it. In this temple was a holy place, where none but the High Priest might enter, and they brought the ark, which had accompanied the children of Israel in all their wanderings, into the holy place. The ark contained the two tables of stone, on which was written the law given on Mount Sinai. And the Shechinah—the glory of the Lord—filled the temple, and all Israel rejoiced in the favor of the Lord. But after a time they became disobedient and sinful, and the glory began to depart from their nation. Jerusalem was several times conquered, and the temple plundered, defaced, and partially destroyed. It was often restored by the Jews. Herod beautified it greatly, but its magnificence was much inferior to Solomon's temple. It was this temple that was visited by our Saviour.

"In the seventieth year of the Christian era the city was entirely destroyed by Titus. The temple, in which many of the unfortunate Jews had taken refuge, was besieged for a long time, and finally destroyed by fire; hundreds of the people perishing in the flames, or rushing out only to be butchered by the Romans.

"For fifty years after this we hear nothing of the temple; then the Roman Emperor Adrian built, on the site of the ancient temple, one he dedicated to Jupiter. This temple was destroyed in some one of the numerous revolutions which took place afterwards in the city.

In 362 the Jews attempted to rebuild the temple, but were frightened from their work by strange prodigies. Flaming swords appeared in the sky over their heads; balls of fire issued from the ground, and rolled among the workmen, doing much damage, and various other wonderful things happened. These things were probably the result of natural causes, of which we know nothing, but they effectually stopped the work.

"In the middle of the sixth century, Justinian built a church here, which was dedicated to the Virgin Mary. The mosque of El-Aksa is supposed to have been this church.

"In 636 the followers of Mohammed, under Omar, took possession of the holy city. Omar was a caliph, or king, and father-in-law to Mohammed. He thought it would be a fine thing to build a mosque on the spot where the great Jewish temple had been. He inquired of the people, in order to find out the exact spot. They tried to deceive him by showing various places, but the old caliph was not to be cheated, and finally he was conducted to the sacred rock, as it was called. This rock, known as Es-Sukrah, was invested with a great many traditions, both by Christians and Mohammedans. The former believed that it had once stood under the holy of holies; and also that it was the very stone that Jacob used for a pillow. They likewise thought it was the spot where the destroying angel stood when about to smite Jerusalem with pestilence. The Arabs have a variety of legends, connecting this rock with their prophet. Over the rock Omar erected his mosque, which is generally known by his name, although Mohammedans call it Haram-esh-Sherif (the Sanctuary).

"Some four or five centuries after this the Crusaders swept down upon the country like a swarm of locusts. After rivers of blood had been spilt, the Christians got possession of Jerusalem. A great number of the Moslem inhabitants took refuge within the mosque of Omar, thinking the invaders would respect that holy place, but their hope was vain. The Christians massacred all indiscriminately, men, women, and children. Those on the roof were shot down with arrows; those in the vaults below the building were drowned in the cisterns; and writers who lived in those days, say that the grounds around the mosque were ankle-deep in blood.

"You are, no doubt, struck with horror at this account of the cruelties of men calling themselves Christians, but you must remember the leaders of these men were only Christians by birthright—that is, they were born in a Christian country, of Christian parents. They had not the grace of God in their hearts. And you must also recollect that the age they lived in was a very barbarous one; and that, bad as these Christians certainly were, from all the accounts which have come down to us, the Mohammedans of that time were even worse.

"After this horrible piece of wickedness had been accomplished to their satisfaction, these inhuman Christians proceeded to clear away the dead bodies, and cleanse the place, and to consecrate the Mohammedan mosque to the worship of the great Jehovah, whose most sacred laws they had been violating. The rock Es-Sukrah they covered with marble, and built an altar over it. The mosque El-Aksa was the residence of King Baldwin II, who there established a new order of knights, called Knights of the Temple. These afterwards became famous throughout Europe, under the name of Knights Templars.

"About a hundred years after these events, the Moslems, led by the famous Saladin, of Egypt, re-conquered Jerusalem. The golden cross was taken down from the mosque, and dragged through the streets. The crescent was elevated in its place, and there it remains to this day. The mosque, the grounds around it, the sacred rock, the subterranean vaults, are all guarded with jealous care by the Moslems, and no infidel is allowed to profane the sacred precincts.

"Thus this beautiful temple area, which lies before us, looking so still and peaceful, with its palms, and graceful buildings, and quiet fountains, has been the 'holy place' of Jews, Pagans, Christians, and Mohammedans. Many a time has it resounded with the tread of armed men, and horrible deeds have been committed there. Its walls have echoed the praises sung to the great Jehovah, the God of Abraham, of Isaac, and of Jacob; the ground has drunk the blood of the sacrifices offered to Jupiter; our Saviour's feet have trod these courts many a time, on blessed deeds of mercy and salvation; its atmosphere has been redolent with the incense offered to the Virgin Mary; full choirs, in grand and sweet chants, have there worshipped the glorious Trinity; and now we hear from it the musical strain of the muezzins:—'There is no God but God, and Mohammed is his prophet!'

"But the time will surely come when the cross will be lifted in the air above Haram-esh-

Sherif, and from its towers and grounds will arise to heaven the triumphant song of Israel restored."

I took this down in short-hand, and it is word for word as the stranger told it to us.

Your affectionate friend,

PHILIP.

VII.

JERUSALEM, Dec. 22, 18—

MY DEAR HARRY:—

It is night, but I do not feel at all sleepy, and though pretty tired, I will give you an account of all that I have seen during the day, while it is still fresh in my mind. I have my little note-book before me to refer to, should I be at a loss. I have got into the way of carrying it about with me, and occasionally jotting down a thing or two, to help my memory.. It is very easy for me to recollect what I *see*, but not so easy to remember what I *hear*, and, as I promised father to write to you a faithful account of everything, I wish to be particular.

This morning, directly after sunrise, our party and the Fanshawes rode out of the Damascus gate, to make the circuit of the city outside of the walls. As soon as we left the gate we found ourselves in the Valley of Jehoshaphat, or Kedron, as it is sometimes called. We turned our horses' heads to the right; and, if you will consult your map, you can follow us on our route.

We passed some ancient quarries. Mr. Fanshawe says they must have been worked for centuries, they are so extensive. They pass under the city quite to the temple area, and hundreds of rooms have been formed by digging out the stones. It was in these rooms, or caverns, that a great many Jews hid themselves during the destruction of the city by Titus. Travellers sometimes explore these rooms, but it is very dangerous. I would like to see them, but don't fancy going under the ground like a gnome, and don't think we will try it. I am ready for any amount of climbing, but don't like to make a mole or weasel of myself. We next came to the Grotto of Jeremiah. This is underneath a high rocky mound (called here a "tell"). The grotto is more like a cavern. It extends a hundred feet under the mound. In it are little buildings, graves, and holy spots walled off. Ibrahim got lighted tapers, and we descended into—what do you suppose?—a cistern. It was very large, and supported by pillars. We tasted the water, and it was cool. On the top of the hill was a Moslem cemetery.

We rode briskly round the northeastern part of the city, and came out upon the bank of the brook Kedron. It had but little water in it, and, at some seasons, is entirely dry. It looks as if it was never very large. Near St. Stephen's gate there is a small cistern, called Mary's Pool, I know not for what reason. South of this gate is the tomb of Mary. That is, it is supposed to be her tomb, but none of our party seemed to put any faith in the legend. The church was closed, so that we could not enter. It is partly subterranean. The tombs of Joachim, and Anna, and St. Joseph are said to be within it, as well as the tomb of Mary. Close by this is a bridge over the Kedron, and, crossing it, we found ourselves at the foot of the Mount of Olives, under the walls of the Garden of Gethsemane. A venerable looking old monk was just entering a gate, and he very politely admitted us. There are eight very old and decayed looking olive trees in the garden, which are believed by some to be the very same which were here in the time of our Saviour. This is scarcely possible, for, though the olive lives to a very great age, longer than any other tree, it is incredible that a tree should live for eighteen hundred years. These are probably the children of those olives. Besides these old trees, there were a great many young ones, which Mr. Fanshawe said had lately been planted. The Latins have possession of this place, and are trying to fix it up like a garden again. Before they took it, it was a bare spot of ground, with the eight trees in it.

After leaving the garden, we soon came to a cluster of four tombs—those of Jehosaphat, Absalom, St. James, and Zacharias. The tombs of Jehosaphat and St. James are excavations; those of Zacharias and Absalom monuments. That of Absalom is very handsome. The lower part is a great block of stone, and has columns cut on all four sides. Above this is a small block, with a dome on it, which has a very pretty ornament on the top. The tomb of Zachariah is like this, except it is differently finished at the top. It is not likely that the persons whose names are given to these tombs were buried in them. Indeed, it is not even pretended that St. James was. The tradition is that he retired within this cave, and spent the time between the crucifixion and the resurrection of Christ.

A little further on we came to the Fountain of the Virgin. This is a well, which looks like a cavern. We went down into it, which is a very easy thing to do, as there are steps all the way down. First, we went down sixteen steps, then we came to a level platform, and then went down twelve more steps. The water was not deep, but clear, and tolerably good, though it had a slightly salt taste. Those persons who make use of this well go down all these steps, and dip up the water in their jars or pitchers, which they then carry off on their heads. They are mostly women.

A little to the south we found the Pool of Siloam, or Shiloh. It is a small, deep reservoir. The water does not stand in it, but flows through, and it is led off by a little channel to water the gardens near by. The water comes by a subterranean passage from the Fountain of the Virgin. You are familiar with the name of this pool. Father found me all the places in the Bible where it is mentioned, and I was surprised that there were only three. It is mentioned in Isaiah as having softly flowing waters; in Nehemiah it is called the dragon well; and in the ninth chapter of John there is the account of our Saviour healing the blind man. We discovered that the name "dragon well" is still given to it by the common people, and the reason is this. The waters flow irregularly, sometimes suddenly becoming deeper and stronger, and more rapid, and then almost ceasing. The common people believe that a dragon lives in the fountain; when he is awake he stops the water, when he is asleep it flows. Near the fountain is the little village of Siloam.

South of this pool is another well, called En-Rogel, and also the well of Job. This is very deep. It is prettily situated among gardens and olive groves. It is a very ancient well, and is mentioned in the book of Joshua.* There is a building over the well. The water is drawn up by hand, in leather buckets, and emptied into stone reservoirs.

West of this is a small hill, called the Mount of Offence, because tradition says this is the hill on which Solomon built altars to false gods.†

We now left the Valley of Jehosaphat, and entered that of Hinnom, passing along at the foot of the hill called the Mount of Evil Counsel. The legend is, that the house of Caiaphas, in which the Jews met to take counsel to destroy Jesus, stood on this hill.‡ On the side of it, not far from the well of Job, they pointed out to us an ancient cemetery, said to be Aceldema, or "Field of Blood," bought with the thirty pieces of silver.

Farther up the valley we came to another pool, called by the Arabs, Birket-es-Sultan; and some distance to the northwest of this, nearly west of the Jaffa gate, there was another, called Birket-el-Mamilla. These are supposed

* 1 Joshua xv. 7. † 1 Kings xi. 7. ‡ Matt. xxvi. 3, 4.

to be the Upper and Lower Pools of Gihon* (for this part of the valley is often called Gihon). The upper pool is large, and the waters are conducted by a small aqueduct to the Pool of Hezekiah, which is within the walls. North of this pool is a Moslem cemetery. From here we rode at a brisk pace to the Damascus gate, for men and horses were getting terribly hungry. As for the ladies, you know they never get hungry. Thus we had made the entire circuit of the city.

After dinner, we found ourselves so far rested that we resolved to sally forth for a walk. I don't know that I have told you in what street "our house" is situated. It is in the Latin Quarter, in a short street leading from the Via Dolorosa, and near the Church of the Holy Sepulchre. We have not yet visited the interior of this famous church. But to return to our walk. We went along the Via Dolorosa, passed the Pool of Hezekiah, and directed our course towards the Gate of Zion. The Pool of Hezekiah is large, but not deep; it was nearly full of water, brought from the Upper Pool of Gihon.†

We turned a little out of our way to visit the Tower of David, which is close by the Jaffa

* Isaiah vii. 3: 2 Kings xviii. 17. † 2 Kings xx. 20.

gate. I don't know why this is called the Tower of David. It was built by Herod, and he named it Hippicus, after his friend. It looks as if it had stood for a thousand years, and might stand for a thousand more.

Passing out of the city, through the Zion gate, we soon came to the house of Caiaphas. We had already been shown *one* house of Caiaphas, and were rather surprised to find another. One was probably his summer residence. This was a poor looking establishment for a high priest to have, but we went in, and beheld some precious relics. Among other things, we saw the stone that closed the door of the sepulchre! We were shown the precise spot where the cock stood which crowed three times during Peter's denial of the Lord! I expect the monks have told these stories so often they now actually believe them. They looked as if they did.

Near by is an American cemetery, which we had not time to visit, as the Tomb of David claimed our attention. This tomb is now converted into a mosque. Whether or not it be the veritable Tomb of David no one can say, for the Mohammedans will not allow any one to visit the tomb. They hold it in great reverence, and guard it jealously. We were allowed to enter the room over the tomb. It is called the Cœnaculum, and is said to be the place where our Lord celebrated the passover with his disciples, and where the Lord's Supper was instituted. It is also said to be the room in which the disciples were assembled on the day of Pentecost. Since I have been in Jerusalem, I have learned to be very doubtful of what they tell me in regard to these sacred places, but father says that fourteen hundred years ago this place is mentioned by Cyril, a Christian bishop. It was then a Christian church, called the Church of the Apostles, and Cyril spoke of it as a received fact, that it was in this place that the cloven tongues descended. So it is likely this tradition is true. Don't you think so?

The room is built of stone. It is sixty feet long, and thirty wide. It is very bare and dreary looking. At one end there is a recess in the wall, where the Christians celebrate mass; at the other end is another recess, where the Mohammedans say their prayers. Queer mixture, is it not? I had a great curiosity to go into the tomb, but I don't believe there is anything in it worth seeing. At a little distance is the English cemetery, but we could not visit it, as the sun was about setting, and we hastened to get into the gate before it was closed for the night.

As this letter is short, I will send you a brief history of Jerusalem, which Hartley wrote for me:—

"We do not know when Jerusalem was founded. It was formerly called Salem, which signifies 'Peace.' It is mentioned in the Bible in connection with Melchisedec,* who, according to ancient tradition, was its founder. Another tradition says he lived in the time of Shem, son of Noah. If so, Jerusalem is the oldest city in the world. Mount Moriah, the scene of the sacrifice of Isaac, was afterward included in the city.

"After this, we hear no more of Jerusalem for five centuries. Then the Israelites, under Joshua, entered the promised land. Jerusalem was one of the cities of the Jebusites, and, in the division of the land, their country fell to Benjamin; but Jerusalem, or Jebusi, as then called, was on the border between the two tribes of Judah and Benjamin, and considered common to both.† But the Jebusites were never completely subdued and expelled from the city, until the time of David. He made it the capital of the country. Here Solomon reigned, and built the temple and palaces, and many other buildings, and was a very magnifi-

* Genesis xiv. 18. † Joshua xv. 8.

cent king. The renown of the city spread to the ends of the earth. Its decline dates from the death of Solomon.

"I cannot record the numerous wars which took place in Judah, and the sieges Jerusalem sustained, until its total destruction by the Babylonians, under Nebuchadnezzar, 580 B. C The city and the temple were destroyed by fire, and the silver, gold, and brass were taken off as spoils, and the Jews carried away captive to Babylon.

"It is a curious fact, that no mention is made, in either sacred or profane history, of the fate of the Ark of the Covenant. We know it was not taken away by the Babylonians; or, if it was, it is the only part of the desecration of the temple which is passed over in silence. We cannot suppose it was burned, as the precious materials of which it was composed would have proved too great temptations to the Babylonians. The Jewish legend is, that the Ark is miraculously preserved in a secret chamber, difficult of access, prepared by Solomon in the sacred rock, which rock is now within the great mosque at Jerusalem. It was deposited there by Josiah, under Huldah, the prophetess. The early Christian Church had another legend They said it was concealed by Jeremiah, the prophet, in obedience to a divine command, shortly before the destruction of the city, in a cave under Mount Nebo, where, with the tabernacle and altar of incense, it is to be preserved until the Lord shall gather his people together again, and receive them into mercy. You can adopt either of these that you may prefer.

"During the reign of Cyrus, the Persian, fifty thousand Jews were permitted to return to Jerusalem, to rebuild the temple. The foundation was laid amid tears and rejoicings; but there were many interruptions to the building, caused by the ill-will of the Samaritans, and it was not till the reign of Darius that the temple was finished and dedicated. Sixty years after this Ezra came, and found the Jews in a state of disorder, owing to their intercourse with their neighbors. This he remedied. Soon Nehemiah came, with authority to rebuild the walls of Jerusalem. The great work which Ezra accomplished, was the collecting together of all the books of the Bible which had then been written.

"When Alexander the Great overthrew the power of the Persians, and became the conqueror of the world, he was very angry with Jerusalem, because its inhabitants had shown sympathy with the Persians, whose monarchs had granted them many favors. Alexander, Josephus says, marched with his army against

Jerusalem, but, as he approached the gate, a wonderful sight met his eyes. The whole population of the city came forth to meet him, clothed in white—the priests in their garments of fine linen, headed by the high priest, dressed in his robes of purple and scarlet, and with his mitre, on which was inscribed the name of the Almighty. Alexander, to the amazement of all his train, prostrated himself before that name, saluted the high priest, and promised protection to the holy city. He then entered the temple, and had sacrifices offered to God, and listened to the prophecies relating to himself, which the high priest read to him out of the Scriptures. The glory and success predicted for him in these prophecies so flattered him, that he gave to the worshippers of this strange God the privileges they asked—permission to worship the God of their fathers, and release from tribute on every seventh year.

"After this the Jewish people came under the power of one nation and another, with various good and evil fortune, until the Syrian monarch, Antiochus Epiphanes, possessed himself of the city. He stripped the temple of its sacred vessels, the palaces were burned, and the walls thrown down. But what was more terrible to the Jews, he interfered with their religious practices. On the altar of the Temple swine (which are an abomination to the Jews) were offered, and temples of idol worship were erected, and daily sacrifices of swine ordered to be offered in them. The religious practices of the Jews were forbidden, and the most horrible tortures inflicted on those who persisted in worshipping the God of their fathers according to the precepts of the Bible. The greater part of the nation gave way and yielded to these impositions, but many remained steadfast.

"And now appeared on the stage the wonderful family of the Maccabees, as they are called. This family consisted of a priest, Mattathias by name, and his five sons, of whom the most distinguished were Simon and Judas. They were citizens of Modin, a town near Jerusalem. The sufferings of their countrymen roused their pity and their indignation. They refused to forsake their religion. Mattathias openly disobeyed the decree of Antiochus ordering him to offer sacrifice to idols. They were all obliged to hide in the deserts to escape the fury of Antiochus and of their apostate countrymen. There they were joined by other Jews who could not be induced by bribes or threats to forsake the worship of the Almighty. The Maccabees organized these men into companies of soldiers. Antiochus sent a division of his army against them. This division came upon a thousand of the Jews, who were dwelling in caves with their wives and children. Now it happened to be the Sabbath-day, and the Jewish laws being very strict with regard to the observance of the Sabbath, these devout Jews thought it wrong to fight on that day. They therefore remained quietly in their caves while their enemies made large fires in front of them, and every soul, men, women and children, were smothered. The Maccabees were not with this devoted band, and they and their followers concluded that after that, though they would make no attack on the Sabbath, they would defend themselves if attacked.

"From this time commenced the renowned exploits of these famous champions. They demolished idol altars, they insisted upon the observance of all religious ordinances, and battled more fiercely against the apostasy of their country than against the Syrians and Macedonians. In the first battle they fought, the Syrian Governor was defeated and slain. Army after army was sent against them only to be discomfitted and routed. Their victories were almost miracles. At one time, with a force of only three thousand, they succeeded, by stratagem, in dividing an army of fifty thousand into three divisions, and then separately defeated them all. At another, with ten thousand soldiers, they completely routed sixty five thousand, led by Lysias, a famous Macedonian general. Five thousand of Lysias' soldiers were slain.

"After fighting a good many battles the Maccabees gained possession of Jerusalem. They cleansed and purified the Temple and restored the ancient worship. A great festival was held on the day the Temple was reopened for the daily sacrifice. This was called the 'Feast of the Dedication,' and it was ordained that it should be annually observed in the Jewish church. This was honored by our Saviour himself, and it is still observed in the synagogues as the 'Feast of Lights.'

"Mattathias died a natural death, but his five sons all came to a violent end. Some were slain on the field of battle and others murdered.

"For a few years after the death of the last of the Maccabees the country was in tolerable quiet. Then civil war broke out; and, while the Jews were fighting among themselves, the Romans marched into their country and put an end to the commotion by conquering the whole of it.

"When our Saviour was born Judea was under the Roman power and Herod was king, but subject to the Roman emperor. This Herod was one of the most wicked and cruel men that ever lived. It is not necessary to relate here all his numerous crimes. That mentioned in Matthew—the slaughter of the infant children of Bethlehem—will give you an idea of his character. While Christ was still a little child Herod was seized with a terrible disease and died in the most awful agonies. His son, Archelaus, was king for nine years, and after that Judea was ruled by Governors. During the time our Saviour was teaching in Judea, Pontius Pilate was governor. He condemned Christ to be crucified.

"But the Jews were not a people to tamely submit to be ruled by another nation. Revolts were common. Especially were they jealous of any act of contempt for their religion, or any interference with it. Quarrels with the Roman governors and Roman soldiers were frequent. At last the Roman emperor, wearied out with the numerous insurrections in Judea, determined to conquer the Jews, and force them to abject submission, or else utterly destroy the nation. Then followed the most horrible of all the horrible wars on record. It is difficult to tell which showed themselves most treacherous and cruel, the Romans or the Jews. The Jews committed all their barbarities under the name of religion, and it is true that they were very zealous for what they called religion—the forms and observances of the Jewish church—and many suffered martyrdom rather than give up one article of their faith. But the religion which would treacherously break the most solemn oaths and massacre the enemies whom the fortune of war threw into their hands, was certainly not that taught by Christ half a century before, in the streets and through the towns and fields where this terrible war was raging.

"It ended in the desolation of the whole country of Judea and the utter destruction of Jerusalem.

"This happened forty years after the crucifixion.

"The siege of the city occurred at the time of the Passover, when vast numbers of Jews from other countries were shut up in the city. This, of course, made provisions very scarce after awhile, although vast stores had been accummulated. Over a million died of famine before the city surrendered. A million and a half were slain during the siege and in the massacres which followed the surrender, when the hapless inhabitants were given up to the fury of the Roman soldiers. A hundred thousand Jews were carried away captive by Titus the conqueror.

"Thus the prophecies of our Saviour in regard to the desolation of the city were all fulfilled. Since then the Jews have been scattered over the whole world. Never since that memorable siege have they assembled in their Holy City for their grand Temple worship. Their beloved country has passed into the hands of strangers, who treat them with scorn when they ask even the poor privilege of going to the walls of Jerusalem to weep over their desolate city. But we know that they will return, for God hath spoken it. In his own good time he will bring it to pass. Then Jerusalem shall become more glorious than of old, and her children shall be gathered to her out of every nation under heaven.

"The Christians were not in Jerusalem during the siege. Believing in the prophecies of Christ they knew its destruction was inevitable; and, being warned, they had all departed long before.

"When the great Roman empire, which claimed the whole of the then known world, fell apart, because of its own weight, Palestine was included in the Eastern empire, and came under the domain of Constantine. You remember how he became converted to Christianity by seeing a flaming cross in the sky, on which were inscribed the words:—'By this sign shalt thou conquer.' It is probable his mind had been opened to receive the truths of Christianity before. He and his mother, Helena, took Palestine under their particular charge. They showed their zeal by erecting costly buildings over all the sacred localities they could discover, or that they imagined they had discovered—for they appear to have been very credulous. Helena was eighty years old when, in 326, she set out for Palestine.

"The first object of her ambition was to discover the cross. But there was no mark or tradition among Christians as to where it lay. But the people of Jerusalem told Helena the cross would certainly be found near the sepulchre, as it was the custom among the Jews to make a great hole near the place where the body of the criminal was buried, and to throw into it whatever belonged to his execution. So Helena set workmen to digging for the sepulchre. A heathen emperor had caused a statue of Venus to be placed on the spot where he was told the sepulchre was, in order to show his scorn for the Christian religion. The workmen irreverently threw down this statue, and after digging to a great depth the sepulchre was discovered. Or, at least, *a* sepulchre was discovered. Tradition said it was the very sepulchre in which Christ had lain. Helena believed it to be the true one, and a great many wise and good men hold that belief to the present time. But there are a great many men, just as wise and good, say the thing is impossible, and they think they can prove it. This dispute, I fear, will last to the end of time, and meanwhile all persons are allowed to take whichever side is to them most agreeable.

"Not far from the sepulchre three crosses were discovered, which Helena immediately supposed were those of Christ and the two thieves. If not those crosses, what ones could they be? The next step to be taken was to discover which of these was the true cross. In regard to this writers are not exactly agreed. Some say the true cross was discovered by Pilate's inscription on it, while others affirm that it was tested by the miracles it worked; first it was applied to a noble lady, who was instantly cured; then to a dead body, which was immediately restored to life.

"Constantine caused a magnificent church to be built over the sepulchre, which was called the Church of the Holy Sepulchre. This was finished in 335, and destroyed by the Persians in 614. Fifteen years after it was rebuilt. This was demolished in 1010 by order of the caliph Hakim. It was rebuilt thirty years after, which building met with the same fate as its predecessors in 1808. Another building was immediately commenced, and this is the edifice which now attracts visitors from all parts of the world.

"But I have wandered away from Constantine's church. When this was consecrated the true cross was placed in it, enclosed in a rich silver case. It was afterward divided into three parts, and deposited in churches in the cities of Jerusalem, Constantinople and Rome. That which was left at Jerusalem was shown to the pilgrims, who were sometimes permitted to break off pieces of it; and, in this way the cross was spread throughout the earth, and yet it never grew less! The inscription was placed in a leaden case and fastened in the top of an arch at Rome, where it remained as late as 1492. The sponge which was dipped in gall and vinegar, and the spear with which the side of Christ was pierced, were found somewhere and sent to Rome; and the crown of thorns was also found and sent to Constantinople, and afterward given to the king of France. The three nails which were in the hands and feet were discovered by Helena. One she threw into the sea on her return voyage home to allay a storm, which threatened to shipwreck the vessel. Of course the storm instantly ceased. Another was sent to Rome, and the third was given to Constantine, who had it placed in his crown."

"The old monk, from whose book I have

copied what I have written regarding these wonderful relics, concludes in these words:—The blood of Christ, which is kept at some places, of which the most famous is that of Mantua, seems to be what has sometimes issued from the miraculous bleeding of some crucifix when pierced in derision by Jews and Pagans, instances of which are recorded as authentic histories. It seems strange that even such a person as our simple-hearted old monk, who lived some three hundred years ago, should have believed such a mass of absurd fables, and yet I am told that these legends are credited by many people at the present day! To Protestant ears they sound almost blasphemous.

"I have devoted quite a space to these things because the Church of the Holy Sepulchre is so identified with modern Jerusalem, and has been the cause of so much speculation, and has given to the world so many learned treatises, that it seemed to merit more than a brief notice

"Thus, under Constantine, Jerusalem became a Christian city; containing Christian churches and was governed by a Christian bishop, which state of things continued for many years.

"In the meantime a new religion had been founded by that wonderful man and cunning deceiver, Mohammed. His followers, every day becoming more powerful, were fast conquering Asia. Having subjugated all the countries about they cast their eyes on Palestine, the possession of which country had indeed been a great object with them all the time, because it was to them a sacred country, being the 'promised land' of Abraham, who was their ancestor as well as that of the Jews. Therefore, one pleasant day, the caliph Omar, at the head of his army, rode up to the gates of Jerusalem. I very much doubt whether any one of the numerous conquerors of Jerusalem had cut such a figure. He was mounted on a camel. From each side of this beast dangled a leathern bag, one filled with fruit, for his own use, and the other with corn, for the camel. Behind him was a leather bottle and a wooden dish. He was dressed in a camel's hair garment, which was decidedly the worse for wear. But he was father-in-law to Mohammed, a man of genius and a great general, though he did choose to sit on the ground instead of a cushion, and to eat off a wooden dish instead of a golden plate. He took peaceable possession of the city, because there was no one to oppose him. He promised to protect both Christians and Jews in their religion, and I am happy to be able to say he kept his word.

"The city continued in the possession of the

Moslems until it was conquered by the Crusaders. They held it for many years, when it was reconquered by the Moslems under Saladin. From that time it has been under Moslem rule.

"Jerusalem has been eighteen times taken, seventeen times sacked and laid in ruins."

Your affectionate friend,

PHILIP.

VIII

JERUSALEM, DEC. 26. 18—.

MY DEAR HARRY:—

In my last I gave you an account of my adventures up to the evening of the twenty-second. The twenty-third was devoted to the Church of the Holy Sepulchre. The strange history connected with this church I also gave you in my last letter. It is an immensely large building, or rather group of buildings, for there are several churches under one roof. They are arranged in the form of a cross. The western part is circular and has a domed roof. Within the church every scene connected with the crucifixion and resurrection of Christ is pointed out, from the spot where he was nailed to the cross, to the place where the crosses were said to have been discovered by Helena.

Directly opposite the door of entrance the first thing you see is the Stone of Unction. It is a marble slab, and on it, tradition says, our Lord's body was laid, and wrapped in linen and perfumed with spices, before being placed in the sepulchre. On one side, near the door, is a flight of eighteen steps. These lead to a chapel on the top of a rock twenty feet above the floor of the church. This rock is Golgotha. It is now covered with marble. In the marble is a hole cut; looking down you can see a small deep hole in the solid rock, where, it is said, the cross was placed. Near this is another hole in the marble, through which you can see that the rock has a crevice with rough sides. This break in the rock we were told happened when the "rocks were rent," at the time of the crucifixion. Coming down from Golgotha, and going up the aisle toward the east, you come to a wide staircase leading down by twenty-nine steps to a chapel, belonging to the Armenians, where they show the throne of St. Helena; this is a stone chair. Thirteen steps below this is a cave where the crosses were discovered. On the northern part of the church is the Chapel of the Apparition, where Christ appeared to Mary Magdalene after the resurrection. On the floor of the church, near the southern part, are marks showing the places where the Virgin Mary and St. John stood during the crucifixion. Within the rotunda, under the dome, is the Chapel of the Sepulchre; this is divided into two chapels, one contains the sepulchre, which belongs to the Latins; the other contains the stone on which the angel was sitting when the disciples visited the tomb; this belongs to the Greeks and Armenians. There are two little wooden chapels close to these, belonging to the Syrians and Copts. The Syrian chapel contains the tombs of Joseph of Arimathea and Nicodemus.

Within the Chapel of the Sepulchre is the rocky cave in which our Lord was buried. Helena had the hill cut away all around it, so that the cave stands out prominently. You cannot see the original rock, for it is all covered with marble. It was done to prevent people breaking off pieces of it. Entering the cave you find yourself in a small square chamber. If you wish to know the exact size I can tell you; six feet eight inches long, six feet one inch wide, and eight feet six inches high. Half the room is occupied by the altar, which covers the real spot where the body of Christ was laid. Lamps are kept constantly burning within the cave.

There are galleries in the rotunda. The dome is full of great holes. The Greeks and Latins have been quarreling about it for several years as to which shall have it repaired; and in the meantime the wind and rain have it all their own way.

Father thinks that the church covers the real Calvary, where Christ was crucified, and also the place where he was buried; but he does not believe in all the sacred places that are shown there. There have been many books written by good men on both sides of the question. Whether this church is really on Calvary or not, I could not stand by the hole in the rock or inside of the sepulchre without feelings of reverence and awe such as I never felt before. The very fact that they have been believed in for ages, that millions of pilgrims, that many holy men, have knelt and worshipped there with joy, it seems to me would make any Christian feel an affection for the place.

We have refrained from going to Bethlehem until the twenty-fourth, as we wished our first visit there to be on the anniversary of our Saviour's birth. William Fanshawe went there on the twentieth and engaged rooms for us at the convent. He could only procure very poor accommodations, for the monks expected the building to be crowded. The Roman Catholics hold a festival on the night of the twenty-fourth, which attracts a great many people.

We rode out of the Jaffa gate at five o'clock in the afternoon. There were twelve in our party, four of them ladies. We were all quite excited, and there was a great deal of lively talking and laughing. Bethlehem is only five miles from Jerusalem, but we were more than two hours reaching it. The road is tolerably good, though rocky in some places; but the air was so soft and pleasant that we were glad to ride slowly, which we were compelled to do anyway, for the road was crowded with people, some walking, some on mules, others on horses; not a vehicle of any kind of course. They were a motley crowd and some very curious looking people among them.

We passed Rachel's tomb, and as we approached Bethlehem we became more quiet and subdued. The stars came slowly out one by one. I know what everybody was thinking of though not a word was spoken. At last Mrs. Fanshawe began to sing "When marshalled on the nightly plain," and we all joined her. We then stopped on a little hill and sang "Glory to God in the highest," and the hymn, "While shepherds watched their flocks by night." Quite a crowd gathered around us, and when we had done singing we led the way into the village, for a long train of Arabs and Armenians followed us.

We found the convent crowded, and supper ready. This was poor enough, but by this time I was so excited that I did not care to eat. But the noise of the crowd around me was disagreeable, and I longed to get into the church, where I thought it would be quiet. After supper we went to the chapel, which is a small building inside the convent walls. The organist was playing as we entered. The music was very fine, no doubt, but did not suit a church in Bethlehem on Christmas Eve. There were opera airs, polkas and waltzes, and I am sure I heard a jig! The congregation meanwhile were amusing themselves with talking and laughing; and, as I had nothing else to do, I looked at the ladies, as I had often been told since I came to Palestine that Bethlehem is celebrated in modern times for the beauty of its women. Well, they are handsome, but they look too much alike. All have large dark eyes, very much like those of gazelles; black hair, olive complexions, large mouths, very red lips, and very white teeth. I like it better in America, where no two women look the least alike. But our ladies don't dress as becomingly as these Bethlehem girls. They wear gay scarfs and ribbons, and the prettiest little red caps.

After a long time some priests made their appearance, and moved about among the crowd, and directly the whole church was a blaze of light; every window was illuminated, and in every place where a lamp could be put there was a light. It had a pretty effect.

The priests began to sing in Latin, but very few of the congregation took any part in the services; they were, most of them, spectators, like ourselves, I suppose. After twelve o'clock something was reverently brought in, taken by the head priest, and held up, while all the people bowed their heads to it. And what do you think it was? A little wooden baby, about a foot long! They call it Bambino, and say it represents the infant Christ. The lights were handed round to the congregation. I took one, as I always like to have a hand in everything that is going on. The priest, with the Bambino in his arms, descended into the grotto below the church, the other priests followed him; and then the whole congregation went down in a long file, bearing torches. Thirteen stone steps lead into the grotto, which is cut in the rock. It is small, and lighted with golden lamps, hung from the ceiling. When the crowd came with their torches there was such a scorching blaze of light, and such great heat, that I nearly suffocated.

At one end of the grotto there is a small recess, in which are twelve lamps, burning constantly. These represent the twelve apostles. In the floor of this recess is a silver star, which marks the spot where Christ was born. In the side of the grotto is another recess, which is the place of the manger, where he was laid. The head priest carried the Bambino to the recess where the star was, and held it there, while he chanted in Latin, the people keeping very still. Then he carried it to the manger, and laid it carefully and reverently inside, and we all ascended to the chapel, and from that to the convent, leaving the wooden baby to its rest in the manger until morning, when it was put away until the next Christmas. The whole thing seemed to me a very ridiculous fuss. There is nothing grand and solemn in such a service. What do you think about it?

Now I suppose it seems strange to you that a place, dug out of a rock, under the ground, should ever have been used as a stable, but father says it is very common in Palestine, even in these days, and, according to ancient writers, was much more common in the days of our Saviour. He says we cannot know whether Christ was born in that exact spot, but the place could not have been far off.

The convent was founded by Jerome. We were shown the cell in which he lived for many years, and wrote books.

We had to sleep on hard straw mattresses, put on narrow iron bedsteads, and were, therefore, up early the next morning. At sunrise father and I were on a little hill, east of the village, where it is said the announcement of Christ's birth was made, to the shepherds. Father told me to look around carefully, and remember every spot, for there was not such another interesting landscape in the world.

About a mile from us was the building which covered the tomb of Rachel. In the plain below us was the field in which Ruth gleaned after the reapers, and where Boaz met her. Near us was the wilderness where John the Baptist preached, and the Valley of Elah, where David slew the giant. In the village at our feet David was annointed king by Samuel, the prophet. In the valley, to the north of us, the hosts of Sennacharib's army were encamped when they were destroyed by the angel of the Lord. And, more wonderful than all these things, and nearer and dearer to our hearts, in the stable of an inn in the little village was born the Saviour of the world. It was a pleasant spot in which to spend Christmas morning.

We returned to the city that afternoon. We passed by the convent of John the Baptist, which stands on the spot where it is said he was born.

This morning we took another ride in the opposite direction from Bethlehem. We rode out of St. Stephen's gate, across the Valley of

Jehosaphat, past the garden of Gethsemane, crossed the little bridge over the Kedron. Here we left our horses, and followed a footpath which led up the Mount of Olives to the Church of the Ascension. The mountain contains three ridges: on the highest of these is the church, or, rather, *was* the church, for now it is a ruin. It professes to mark the spot from which Christ ascended into heaven. A mosque stands near these ruins, and there we got the key of the church. We found ourselves first in an open, paved court, around which were various altars, belonging to different Christian sects. In the centre of the court is a small building, which the Mohammedans use for prayer. Before this is the rock from which tradition tells us Christ ascended. There is a footprint in the rock, which is, by some, asserted to be Christ's, but I doubt whether this is generally believed, though the pilgrims, who flock to these holy places, are most of them excessively ignorant.

After leaving the church we were shown the Cave of the Creed, an underground room, cut in the rock. Here it is said Christ used to teach his disciples. Farther down the mountain we came to the spot where it is said Jesus taught his disciples the Lord's prayer. Then we visited the Tombs of the Prophets. A long underground gallery leads you into a large room; from this are three passages, which lead to galleries. In one of these are places for corpses. I don't know why it is called the Tombs of the Prophets. We visited the Jewish cemetery, which is also on this mountain.

The trees are very scattering now on the mountain, but in our Saviour's time it was probably covered with trees, and must have been a delightful place. I don't wonder it was the favorite resort of Christ and his disciples. Even now it is a very pleasant spot, and from it you get fine views of the holy city. We could see the Dead Sea in the distance. Some of the olive trees looked as if they might be centuries old. We rambled about for some time, and then, as our scattered forces collected together, we mounted our horses and took the road round the hill, over the side of the Mount of Offence, which road, you will see, leads to Bethany.

This is two miles from Jerusalem, and, as the route we were taking is the only regularly travelled route, and has been from the oldest times, we were in the very path that Christ took when he rode toward Jerusalem, the people strewing palm branches in his way.

Bethany is a little village of some thirty houses. The monks showed us the house of

Mary and Martha, and of Simon the leper, and the tomb of Lazarus. This last is right in the middle of the village; it is a deep vault. Father says I must put no faith in any of these legends. But it seems hard not to believe things when you want to so very much.

We returned to Jerusalem to dinner, after which father and I visited a very interesting place. It is called the Place of Wailing. It is on the west side of the temple area, outside the walls. The wall in this place is built of very ancient stones, thought to have been part of the temple itself. The Jews have *bought* of the Moslems the right to visit this spot when they please, to weep over the ruin of the temple, and downfall of the nation. We found several Jews there. Some old men seemed to be praying, some were reading Hebrew books. A company of women were kneeling close by the wall, with their heads bowed down, uttering cries and groans. The entrance to this place is through a narrow, crooked alley, which makes it tolerably private.

This morning, before we started for Bethany, we parted with Mr. Elliott. I almost envied him, thinking of his going *home*. But I reflected I had not seen all I wanted to in Palestine. To-morrow we leave Jerusalem. There is much to be seen here yet, but we expect to return, and may make quite a long stay. Our journey will be northward, until we reach the sea of Galilee.

Your affectionate friend,

PHILIP.

IX.

TIBERIAS, Jan. 15, 18—.

MY DEAR HARRY:—

Since my last letter I have taken quite a long journey in a round-about fashion. We arrived at this place this noon. Our tents are pitched on the shores of the lake, just outside the town. And now we are all going to rest, and write letters this afternoon, leaving all explorations until to-morrow. I will tell you something about the most interesting of the numerous places we have seen. I have not had a good opportunity to write during my journey, and shall find my note-book of great service in making out this letter. You must prepare your mind for a long one.

After leaving Jerusalem, the first place we saw in which you could take any particular interest was Gibeon. This place, in the time of Joshua, was a great and mighty city. You remember the trick the inhabitants played off on Joshua, to make him enter into a treaty of peace with them. They took torn and shrivelled-up wine bottles, old sacks, mouldy bread, shoes tied on the feet with cloths, etc., to make the Jews think they came from a long distance, when, in fact, they lived not many miles from Jerusalem. It was near Gibeon that the terrible battle was fought between Joshua and the Jews on one side, and the kings of the land on the other, when Joshua commanded the sun and moon to stand still, and they obeyed.

Gibeon, or El-Jib, as it is now called, is only a poverty-stricken village, inhabited by Moslems, but there are the remains of ancient buildings of great splendor all round there. Some of these ruins are inhabited, but I think at the risk of broken bones, for loose stones are lying about in every direction, it never having entered into anybody's head to remove them, or restore them to any kind of order. We did not stay long in Gibeon. We drank of the famous fountain, and took a bird's-eye view of Wady Yalo, or the Valley of Ajalon, where the battle was fought. I think, of all the miracles of the Bible, I would rather have seen that than any other, and of all its heroes, I would rather have been Joshua. But if I fill up the letter with my thoughts, I shall never get on.

One day we took our lunch by the fountain near Shiloh, the water of which we found very pure and delicious. Shiloh is where the ark rested for so long a time. It was here that Samuel was dedicated to the Lord, and here Eli lived with his two sons, Hophni and Phineas, who were both so wicked. At that time, probably, it was a gay and lively place; we know there was a yearly festival held there. But there are no festivals held now-a-days in the poor, dingy-looking little village, which is called Seilun.

We spent three days most delightfully in Nabulous, or Nablus. In ancient times this city was called Shechem, and is one of the very oldest cities in the whole world. It lies between two mountains, Ebal on the north, and Gerizim on the south, in one of the loveliest little vallies I ever saw. This valley of Nablus is watered by a small, clear stream, and filled with beautiful gardens, and pretty villages, and orchards of pomegranates, figs, olives, and many other trees. The weather was warm as spring, and numbers of birds were enjoying themselves among the groves, and making everybody happy with their songs. It must be a charming place to spend the summer, when the trees are full of fruits and blossoms, and there are millions of birds. Then, as Ibrahim said to me, "your lips will be kissed by fragrance, and your ears by melody." I think it would be more in accordance with fact, if he had said your nose instead of your lips, as that organ was given us for smelling; but I suppose nose is not considered poetical. Our tents were pitched among the orchards, outside of the city.

Nablus is a queer old place. The city is long, but not very wide; the streets are narrow; the houses high, built of stone, with domes on the roofs. The rocks on the sides of Gerizim overhang the city in some places, and look as if they would topple on the houses. Mounts Ebal and Gerizim are steep, rocky precipices, on each side of the town, eight hundred feet high. They have a very grand and imposing appearance, and make you feel as if they were protectors to the city nestling between them. These were the mounts of blessing and of cursing. In the book of Deuteronomy we have an account how Moses, by the Lord's direction, commanded the people, when they came into the promised land, to build an altar on Mount Ebal. Six tribes were to take their station on that mountain to read the curses of the law, and six on Mount Gerizim, to read the blessings. In Joshua we have the account how all this was done. It must have been a grand scene, with the tents of the Israelites covering the plain; the people assembled in a vast multitude; the Levites on the mountains, alternately reading the blessings and curses, and the whole congregation responding amen! This was after a great and terrible battle, in which the Israelites were entirely victorious.

The most interesting portion of the city is Samaritan's quarter. We visited it several times, and I don't know which asked the greatest number of questions, the Samaritans or ourselves. They were very polite and very talkative, and told us a great many remarkable things, all of which they firmly believe. There are not more than a hundred and fifty of them, all told, and when I asked a young man if that was all of his nation left in the world, he said, "Yes, all that are in the parts of the world that could be visited." To be sure, there was a colony living beyond the river Sabt, or the Sabbatic River, so called because it can be crossed only every seventh day. Sabbatic means seventh, and as the Jews and Samaritans regard the seventh day as holy, Saturday is their Sabbath. This colony could not be visited by Samaritans on the seventh day, as their religion forbids them to travel on that day. As I was curious to krow why this river could only be crossed on a Saturday, he told me that on every other day in the week the water leaped up with tremendous force, and to a great height, and cast up stones constantly, so that it was dangerous to go near it. I told him then that I would undertake to cross the river, if he would tell me precisely where it was. That he did not know, only it was towards the rising sun. I then asked him why the Samaritans did not get some of their neighbors, who did not keep the seventh day holy, to cross the river for them, and visit their relations. But he only stared, and asked me if I had ever seen any Samaritans anywhere else. You must not suppose I talked directly to this young man, for he spoke Arabic, which I don't know at all. Ibrahim acted as interpreter.

The priest was a good old fellow. He wore a red silk robe and a white turban, and looked very fine indeed. He went with us to their synagogue. We had to take off our shoes before we entered. It is a small room, without ornaments, figures, or pictures. On one side was a little recess, concealed by a curtain. The priest disappeared behind this curtain. Presently he made his appearance again, holding in his hand a couple of rods. Around these a parchment was rolled, and after we had given him some money he unrolled the parchment for our benefit. It was written all over with strange looking characters, and was very musty and very much patched. This manuscript, the priest told us, was three thousand

"The priest was a good old fellow." Page 148.

four hundred and eighty years old, and was written by Abishua, who was the son of Phineas, who, you know, was one of the sons of Eli. When he said this, I am sorry to say, Hartley whistled, but, luckily, the priest was too busy talking to hear him.

Mount Gerizim is the holy mountain of the Samaritans. Three times a year they go up in solemn procession to worship there—at the Feast of Pentecost, the Feast of the Passover, when they pitch their tents on the mountain, and stay all night, offering a sacrifice of seven lambs at sunset, the Feast of the Tabernacles, during which they live on the mountain, in booths made of the branches of trees. We went up the mountain, of course. Two young men went with us as guides. We ascended on the eastern side, where the holy places are. First we came to a small hole in the rock, where the lamb is roasted on the evening of the Passover. Next we came to the ruins of what had once been a very large building. These are supposed by some to be the ruins of the ancient temple of the Samaritans, which was destroyed more than a hundred years before the birth of Christ. If so, the present Samaritans seem to care very little about it. Near this building we were shown some flat stones in a row. Under these, our guides told us, were the twelve stones brought out of Jordan by the Israelites, when they first came into the country,* and there they are to remain until the coming of the Messiah; for the Samaritans, like the Jews, are yet expecting the Saviour, whom they call El-Muhdy, or the Guide. Just beyond these stones is the holy place of the Samaritans. They turn their faces towards it when they pray. Our guides took off their shoes as we approached it. This is the custom in the East, when reverence is to be shown to any place. It is a large, flat, bare rock, even with the ground. Their tradition is, that on this rock the Tabernacle of the Lord, with the Ark of the Covenant, was pitched.

On reaching the top we found the view very fine. We could look over Mount Ebal, which seemed to be very much the same kind of mountain as Gerizim. There is nothing on it of particular interest, I believe.

That evening I asked Hartley to write down all he knew of the Samaritans for your benefit and mine, and here is what he has written:—

"In order fully to understand the history of the Samaritans, we must go back to the revolt of the ten tribes.

"During the latter part of the reign of Solo-

* Joshua iv

mon, when he had forsaken God, and served idols, he began to oppress some of the tribes, and lay unjust burthens upon them. At his death, his son Rehoboam ascended the throne, and the people petitioned him to be less severe with them than his father had been. But he refused, and told them he intended to lay greater burdens upon them. This foolish speech lost him the greater part of his kingdom. Ten tribes immediately rebelled, and chose Jeroboam for their king. Two tribes only, Judah and Benjamin, remained to Rehoboam. He assembled all the fighting men of the two tribes, to make war upon his revolted subjects. But the Lord sent a prophet forbidding him, as this thing was from God. So, for more than two hundred years, there were two kings in Palestine; one over the two tribes, called the King of Judah, and one over the ten tribes, called the King of Israel. The capital of Judah was Jerusalem; the capital of Israel was Samaria. Sometimes these kings would make peaceful alliances with each other, and sometimes they waged terrible war.

"Seven hundred and twenty years before Christ, Shalmanezer, King of Assyria, made war upon Israel, and conquered it. He besieged Samaria three years, and at last got possession of the city, and carried away the king, Hoshea, and all the people of the country, as captives, and compelled them to settle in Media and Persia, while, at the same time, he ordered the inhabitants of Cuthah, in Persia, to settle in Israel. Thus the ten tribes were removed from the 'promised land,' eight hundred years after first taking possession of the country. God permitted this as a punishment for the great wickedness of the nation.

"The people of Cutha, or Cutheans, who had settled in Israel according to the commandment of Shalmanezer, were all idolaters, which was displeasing to the Lord, and he sent lions among them.* These terrified the people so much that they sent word to Shalmanezer that they did not know how to worship the God of the land, and feared they would all be destroyed. Then the king commanded that a priest from among the ten tribes should return and teach the Cutheans how to worship 'the God of the land.' This was done, and ever after they continued to observe the religious worship of the Jews; though it is said in the Bible they secretly worshipped their own gods, and taught their children so.† These people the Jews called Samaritans, from Samaria, the capital of their country.

* 2 Kings xvii. 25. † 2 Kings xvii. 41.

"When the Jews, under Zerubbabel, returned from their exile and began to build Jerusalem and their temple, the Samaritans also desired to aid them in their work: 'Let us build with you, for we seek your God as ye do; and we do sacrifice unto him since the days of Esar-haddon.' It was the refusal of the Jews to admit them to this privilege that gave rise to the ill-will between the two races, and from that time the Samaritans did all they could to hinder the rebuilding both of the temple and the city. It was the same refusal, probably, with other acts of mutual hatred, that induced the Samaritans to erect a temple of their own on Gerizim-Sichem, at the foot of Gerizim, now become the metropolis of the Samaritans. According to Josephus, if a Jew at Jerusalem was accused of eating unclean food, or of breaking the Sabbath, or of any crime, he fled to Sichem, declaring himself to be unjustly accused. Thus there came to be many apostate Jews among the Samaritans. The mutual hatred continued to increase, each party contending for the sanctity of its own temple. At last the temple on Gerizem was destroyed by the Jews, under John Hyrcanus, about one hundred years before Christ. This did not mend matters, and the hatred grew more violent, until, under the procurator Coponius, who followed Archelaus, a Samaritan entered Jerusalem secretly, and polluted the temple by scattering in it human bones. The very name of Samaritan had now become a byword and term of reproach among the Jews, and all intercourse with them was avoided. We have abundant proof of this in the New Testament. Jesus himself was called a Samaritan in scorn; and the seventy disciples, when first sent out, were not to go to any city of the Samaritans, because they did not belong to the house of Israel.

"They still clung to their worship on Mount Gerizim, though they had no temple, and lived in constant expectation of a Messiah.

"Yet, after the crucifixion, many believed on Christ in Sichem itself, and churches were gathered by the apostles in their towns and villages.

"Not long after the times of the New Testament the city of Sichem received the new name of Neapolis, which remains to the present day; under the Arabic form Nabulous.

"In 479, under Zeno, the hatred of the Samaritans broke out against the Christians, and they killed many of them. The Christians complained to the emperor, who caused the Samaritans to be driven from Mount Gerizim, and the Christians built there a church to the Virgin. During the reign of Justinian the Samaritans again rebelled and a battle was fought, in which an immense number of Samaritans were slain. The emperor took away all their synagogues, declared them incapable of public employment or of acquiring property. Many of the people became Christians. From that time the existence of the Samaritans is rarely mentioned in history. Only a small remnant of them remain to this day.

"As for the ten tribes, no one knows what became of them after their settlement in Media and Persia. History is silent on the subject. To what parts of these countries they were carried, and what befell them afterward, we do not know; but, in the absence of any positive information, the wildest fables have been told about them. Some say they emigrated to America, and that the Indians found there on the discovery of the continent were their descendants; others think that their descendants are to be found in the interior of Africa; others say they will be discovered in some continent yet unknown. They are always spoken of as the lost tribes of Israel, and this expresses all we know.

"The two tribes of Judah and Benjamin were hereafter known as but one—that of Judah. The fate of the Jewish nation has been told in the history of Jerusalem."

The next day we visited Jacob's well. It is at the foot of Mount Gerizim, about half an hour's walk from the city. It is a curious fact that Jews, Samaritans, Christians and Mohammedans all believe in the tradition that this is the veritable well of Jacob, and that Joseph is buried near it. Father showed me the account which is given in the last part of the thirty-third chapter of Genesis, how Jacob built near Shechem an altar, which he called El-elohe-Israel, (God the God of Israel), and how he bought a "parcel of a field" of Hamor, Shechem's father. Then he found for me the fiftieth chapter of Genesis, where Joseph charged the children of Israel to carry his bones with them into Palestine. Then in Exodus it is told us that Moses did take the bones of Joseph with him; and in Joshua we find that the Israelites buried the bones of Joseph in a parcel of ground which Jacob bought of the sons of Hamor, so there is no doubt about the identity of the places. This well is mentioned in the New Testament in the fourth chapter of John. An interview took place at this well between our Saviour and a Samaritan woman.

A large stone covered the well. This was removed and we looked down into it. It is some forty feet deep. There was but little water in it. There is a great deal of rubbish lying about near the well, which rubbish is said to be all that is left of a Christian church which once stood there.

We spent a day in Samaria, or, as it is now called, Sebustich, or sometimes Sebustia. Samaria was the capital of the ten tribes after their revolt, and when these tribes were carried away, it was the capital of the Samaritans until they chose Sichem. It is a fine situation for a city—on the top and sides of a hill six hundred feet high. The hill is large, oval in form, and stands right in the centre of a beautiful valley. The valley and hill-sides are very fertile, and are all under cultivation. The view from the top of the hill was, I thought, the most beautiful I had yet seen in Palestine. Below you is the green valley, all around you are high hills, dotted here and there with villages (not dirty Arab hamlets, but quite nice-looking villages), and covered with orchards and vines.

I don't wonder that the city of Samaria was very populous and beautiful, and that Herod the Great took the trouble to build there magnificent temples and castles. This splendid city is now in ruins. Indeed, but very few of the ruins have been left. The stones have been taken to build the houses of the neighboring villages, and the ground has been ploughed and cultivated so carefully that the ruins have gradually disappeared. Those left are mostly colonnades. In several places there are rows of columns. In one we counted nearly a hundred standing upright, and great numbers lying on the ground! O, but that must have been a magnificent colonnade! Father said it could not have been less than fifty feet wide and three thousand long! The capitals are all gone. Without them the columns measure sixteen feet in height and six in circumference. This colonnade is supposed to have been built by Herod the Great, but nobody knows anything about it.

The church of St. John the Baptist is also on the hill. This church is not as old as the ruins I have just been writing about, but it has the merit of being almost entire. It was built during the Crusades, and is said to cover the place where John was beheaded, and also the spot where he was buried. Father says this is very doubtful; but as there seems to be no certainty about where he was executed, I have no objections to believing that this is the place. The church is very large, with high, pointed arches. In it are two small buildings, a mosque (they are everywhere) and the tomb. The last is nothing but a room cut in the solid rock. To get to it we had to go down a flight of steps.

There is a little village on the hill which bears the ugly name of Sebustich. Nearly all the modern names of these places are ugly. They are generally Arabic, and, judging the language by its proper names, it must be a disagreeable one. The houses of the village are well built of the stones the builders found ready cut and ornamented to their hand among the ruins of Herod's palaces. "Sic transit gloria mundi," you know, was one of our Latin copies. The people were cross and surly-looking, and I don't think hurt themselves with over politeness. But we may be thankful they did not do us a mischief, for they have the name of being rather rough to their visitors.

After leaving this hospitable place, we entered upon the plain of Esdraelon. This plain, father told me, extended from the Mediterranean Sea on the west to the valley of the Jordan on the east, and from the hills of Samaria on the south to those of Galilee on the north. It is twelve miles wide at its widest part. It is a beautiful plain, containing many groves of fine trees. In the summer time the fields are filled with luxuriant crops of grain. It is surrounded on all sides by hills, some of which are so high that they are called mountains. There are great numbers of villages in this plain, most of them being situated on the sides of the hills. As we rode through these villages, we frequently met women bearing water-jars on their heads. They carried them easily and walked very gracefully, but never a word would any of them speak to me, though I spoke to them very politely. In fact they seldom looked at us. But the men all stopped and said *salaam*, which means "peace." They say that in place of our "how do you do."

Even in this beautiful plain we saw some dark tents of the wandering Arabs. They settle like locusts, and where they settle every green thing disappears. When the harvest time draws near, they come down upon the fertile plains in swarms, to the great terror of the inhabitants, who see these miserable creatures reap the rich harvests they have taken such pains to bring to perfection. No wonder this beautiful plain is not so well cultivated as it used to be, and that some of the villages are deserted.

I used to read in my story books at home such romances about these Bedouins that I thought they were among the noblest people on the face of the earth. Their kindness to travellers; their generosity to those who had "eaten of their salt;" their tender care of dumb animals, especially horses; their love of truth and honor, and I don't know what beside. But let me tell you, Harry, that all this is mere *fudge.* Why, I used to think it was a pity that nations should become civilized when these half-savage Arabs were so much nobler! But now that I have seen and known these noble, generous, truthful savages, I shall be very thankful when I return to America to find myself among civilized beings. These "noble Arabs" are treacherous, lying, thieving rogues, and more greedy of money than any other race on the globe, which is saying a great deal. There is some little truth in the "eating of their salt" story. That is to say, after you have "eaten of their salt," or, in plain English, been their guest, they only do a moderate amount of cheating and fibbing, and feel bound to protect you from violence, and to keep their hands from picking and stealing your goods. What can be meaner than this way they have of leading idle, vagabond lives all the time industrious farmers are working, and then, when the crops are ready to be gathered, coming in great numbers to steal the ripe grain? So much for the Arabs. They look better in poetry and pictures than anywhere else, because out of the pictures they are very dirty and greasy.

We did not stop at Jezreel. It is a collection of mean little hovels. It is beautifully situated, and when Ahab held his court there, was,

I suppose, a very elegant and fashionable place.

We then rode along the foot of the mountains of Gilboa, to Little Hermon. This is so called to distinguish it from Great Hermon, which, you know, is higher up, where the two ranges of Lebanon meet. The mountain did not look very attractive, being bare and rocky, so we passed by. These mountains of Gilboa have seen some terrible battles. It was here that Gideon and his handful of men overthrew the hosts of the Midianites. Here the Israelites were defeated by the Philistines, and Saul and his three sons were killed. You remember that it was the night before this battle that Saul went to consult the Witch of Endor. I asked father to take me to Endor, but he said there was nothing there to see. There are a great many caves in these rocks, any one of which will answer for a witch's cavern. And, strange to say, people lived in them. Most wretched beings they seemed to be; and, as far as I could judge, the animals they kept lodged in the same cavern with themselves. Those that were standing outside of these miserable abodes shrieked after us as we rode along. I could not understand their language, but Ibrahim said they were swearing at us for Christian dogs.

We passed through the ruined village of Nain, and a ride of four miles further brought us to the foot of Mount Tabor. It is a beautiful mountain, standing by itself, and covered with trees to the very top. From my first view of it, I should think the mountain was nearly round. Its height is a thousand feet above the plain. The path up the side is tolerably good. It took our party about an hour and a half to reach the top. All day long I had been very impatient to reach this spot. I did not want to speak to any one, but I thought with a great deal of pleasure that I was standing on the mount, perhaps on the very spot, where Moses and Elias appeared and talked with Christ.* I was going over the scene in my own mind, and imagining how the disciples looked, and what they said, when Mr. Hamilton brought my flying fancy flat to the ground by saying he did not believe that this was the Mount of Transfiguration, and, in fact, nobody believed it now. That at the time of our Saviour there was a fortified city on it, and that the miracle must have taken place nearer to the Sea of Gallilee. Father immediately took up the argument, and said that the city was no objection to the miracle, as there were plenty of

Matt. xvii. 1-9.

secluded places probably, at a distance from the city, and that it was sufficiently near to the Sea of Gallilee; and that, as it was peculiarly well situated for such a scene, he chose to believe that it actually occurred there. But the fact of there being a *doubt* on the subject, made me lose all interest in the mount as a "sacred place."

If I was surprised to hear that this mountain might not have been the Mount of Transfiguration, I was just as much surprised to find on its summit the ruins of a city. The foundations of a thick wall can be traced all around the top, besides walls, and arches, and parts of dwelling-houses and other buildings. There are also the remains of a fortress. Mr. Hamilton says these ruins belong to different ages, probably most of them to the time of the Crusades. But long before that there was a city there—probably as far back as the time of Joshua. We know, from Roman history, that there was a fortified city here during the time of Christ. In later times the Crusaders built a city and fortress here.

We had many good views from the different sides of Mount Tabor. Far to the north we could see the snowy top of old Hermon; on the northwest we could faintly see the Mediterranean; on the northeast was the Lake of Tiberias. At the foot of the mountain, and stretching away to Mount Carmel, we had a view of the whole plain of Esdraelon, with the Kishon at no great distance, its waters swollen by the winter rains. Around us were villages full of interesting associations, Nain, Jezreel, Endor, Nazareth.

After we had watched the sunset we mounted our horses, and rode slowly down the mountain, and then cantered away to Nazareth, where we arrived after dark, very weary and hungry.

We gave up two days to Nazareth. I found it quite a town, a larger place than I expected to see—I have become so accustomed to little hamlets and mean villages. It contains about three thousand inhabitants. The houses are well built of stone. The people are good-looking, especially the women. I saw some young girls who were quite handsome, but not so pretty as the Bethlehem girls. They were not dressed so becomingly. They wore rolls of old coins around their heads, which seems to me a funny idea. I thought some of our coin collectors in Philadelphia would like to strike a bargain with these Nazarenes; but Ibrahim tells me they can never be persuaded to sell these head-dresses at any price.

Early in the morning of both days we were there, we went to the Chapel of the Annunciation, to hear the monks read mass. The services were very impressive; made more so to me from the fact that nearly all the congregation was composed of the wandering Arabs of the desert who have become converted to Christianity. It seemed strange to see these wild, uncouth-looking figures, in their uncivilized dresses, going through the forms of Christian worship, making the responses in a reverent manner, and joining in the chants. As this is a Roman Catholic church, the service was in Latin; but the first day it was followed by a sermon in the Arabic language, to which the Arabs listened very devoutly.

This church is said, by the Latin Church, to cover the very spot where Mary was when the angel appeared to her to announce the birth of Jesus.

We were shown over the convent to which the chapel is attached. It is a collection of buildings, looking something like a church, but more like a castle. The whole effect is quite grand. The monks are very hospitable to all visitors. They also receive with great kindness any poor unfortunate traveller who has lost his all by the Bedouin Arabs, or who has been driven to their doors by the fierce storms which often prevail in the neighboring mountains. These they comfort with the good things of life, and then send them on their way rejoicing.

As usual, we were shown a great many "sacred places." There was the cave and kitchen of Mary, the workshop of Joseph, the dining-table of our Lord and his disciples, the synagogue where he read the prophet Isaiah,* and, at a distance from the town, the Mount of Precipitation. This last is shown as the place where the people of the city threatened to throw our Saviour over the precipice, but he escaped them.

But I have not told you what we saw in the church. From the entrance, a flight of steps leads down to an altar, which stands in a recess. This recess is said to be the cave in which Mary lived. The walls are now partly covered with marble, and partly showing the natural rock. The marble slab in front of the altar is actually worn with the kisses of the numerous pilgrims who have visited this spot. This marks the exact spot where Mary stood when the angel appeared. On it are the words, "Verbum caro hic factum est." Close by is a broken pillar, which marks the spot where the angel stood. He is supposed to have entered through a hole in the rocky wall. Behind the

* Luke iv. 16.

altar is a narrow passage, which leads into another cave, which is said to have been the residence of a friend of Mary's, who kept house for her when away from home.

We several times visited the "Fountain of the Virgin," as it is now called. This is the only fountain in the place, and the only one it ever had; therefore our Saviour must have visited it constantly. This, then, was a "sacred place" we were *sure* of.

In a field, close by the fountain, was *another* Church of the Annunciation. This belongs to the Greeks, who are never to be outdone by the Latins. They contend that this church covers the cave where Mary lived, and the place where the angel appeared to her. This is in the opposite side of the town from the Latin church. We did not go inside of it; having already seen one cave, we did not care to see another. The outside of the church is dull and mournful enough.

We climbed up a high hill west of the town, for the sake of the view, which is fine. We could see several mountains, Tabor, Little Hermon, Gilboa, Samaria, and, far in the west, Carmel, running out into the sea. We could even distinguish the convent of Elias on its summit. We could see the Mediterranean, too, distinctly, and the bay of Akka. We all concluded that Christ must have often come to this hill, to enjoy the noble prospect. This thought, you may be sure, will make us remember the western hill and its prospect forever.

While we were on the hill, father told to Hartley and me the strange story of the Holy House of Loretto. As you may never have heard it, I will send it to you.

"You have seen *two* churches of the Annunciation, each party, Latins and Greeks, contending that their church contains the cave of Mary. Well, in Italy, on the slope of the Appenine Mountains, overlooking the Adriatic Gulf, there is the *third*. You wonder, probably, how long Nazareth has been in Europe, and how Mary's house happens to be in a country she never even visited, that we know of. This I can explain to you in a satisfactory manner, if you will only believe that in the thirteenth century the house in which Mary lived at the time of the Angel's visit, and where she afterwards resided with her husband and the child—Christ—was taken away from Nazareth by angels, conveyed through the air to France, at the head of the Adriatic Gulf, and that from there it was afterward carried to the plain of Loretto, and from there removed to the hill of Loretto in the same miraculous manner. You think, perhaps, that it would be a hard matter to make any one believe such a wild story as this. And yet, in the whole Christian world, there is not a church so frequented as this at Loretto. The most of these worshippers are persons who religiously believe in this wonderful removal, and who regard the *Santa Casa* (Holy House) as an actual fragment of the Holy Land, and as the very house made sacred forever by the presence of Christ and his parents. The church which contains this *Santa Casa* is very large, and is constantly thronged. A hundred priests are always in attendance, and the church is open from early dawn until far into the night. A hundred and twenty masses are said there daily. When the doors of the church are opened in the morning, two soldiers, with drawn swords, take their places at the entrance of the Santa Casa. The first mass begins, and then the Santa Casa itself is opened and lighted. Then the pilgrims begin to flock in, and from that time until sunset come and go in a perpetual stream. The pavement around the 'House' is deeply worn, because all the pilgrims, from the king to the peasant, crawl around it on their knees. After they have visited the sacred spot where Mary stood (which is marked by a marble slab, with the same inscription that we saw to-day), they retire backward from the church, so that their faces may be kept towards this holy place. All around the walls the story of the wonderful removal of the House is written in all languages, that none may be ignorant of it.

"I talked with the monks this morning about this House at Loretto, and asked them how they reconciled the two stories. They told me that the 'House,' which had been carried to Italy, was certainly the house where Mary and her family resided, and that the cave they showed us was connected with the main building by a passage. They pointed out to me the very spot where the house stood. But those who are learned and have closely examined into this matter, tell us that from the construction of the walls of the House at Loretto, if it could be placed by the cave at Palestine, it would certainly block up the only entrance to it. Furthermore, they tell us that of the many pilgrims who visited Nazareth before this removal by the angels, not one makes any mention of the house of Joseph and Mary being there. They would scarcely omit such an important place. And, besides all this, the 'Santa Casa,' the walls of which can be seen from the inside, though the outside is cased in marble, is built of a dark-red stone, of a kind which is not to be found in all Palestine.

"The reason given for the removal of the 'House,' is that it was desirable to remove it from this land of disorder, and confusion, and savages, to a land where it would be protected by the Roman Catholic church."

Don't you think it is wonderful, Harry, how any one can believe in such wild romances as the above? And yet I suppose some very wise people do believe them. But I must close this letter, which I have spun out to a great length.

Your affectionate friend,

PHILIP.

X.

TIBERIAS, Jan. 29, 18—.

MY DEAR HARRY:—

My last letter was dated from this place, but you are not to suppose we have been here all this time. We have made the circuit of the Lake of Tiberias, or the Sea of Galilee, or Gennesaret, whatever you choose to call it. I prefer the name of the Sea of Galilee.

From the point where I am writing—a high hill near Tiberias—I have a view of the whole lake. It is very small compared with our great lakes, being only thirteen miles long and six wide. There is a fine beach all around it. The water is beautifully clear. The lake is completely shut in by high hills, which give it the appearance of being held in a large, deep basin. There is nothing very beautiful about these hills, except that just now they are covered with the loveliest green. Ibrahim says he has seen snow on the hills at this season, but that it is a rare thing. This winter has been very mild; and, lately, rains have been frequent. There are deep, narrow valleys between these hills, which, I believe I have told you before, are called wadies in this country. There seem to be as many fish in the lake as there were in the time of the apostles. We have feasted on them since we have been here, and found them delicious. I have tried my luck at fishing, with tolerable success. All the fishing is done from the shore. I have not seen a boat on the lake all the time we have been here. Is it not strange? During our Saviour's sojourn on the lake, there were plenty both of boats and ships. But these seem all to have passed away, even as the chariots and wagons from their roads.

I can see from here the place where the river Jordan flows into the lake at the northern end, also the place where it flows out at the south.

I have told you of the beach which encircles the sea. It was on this beach, probably, that most of the scenes recorded in the Bible as happening in Galilee took place. It was here our Saviour stood and told the disciples where to cast their nets when they drew up millions of fishes,* and where Peter walked on the waves.† It was on this beach the multitude stood while Jesus addressed them from the ship. At that time there was a great deal of life, and activity, and trade, and business on the

* Luke v. † Matt. xiv. 29.

beach which is now so quiet; for Herod had built cities on the shores of the lake. But the hills were always desert and solitary, and it was to these the Lord used to retire when he wished to be alone, or have only the company of his disciples.

The greater part of Christ's public life was passed around the shores of this sea, which makes it very interesting to us Christian pilgrims. The western side is principally spoken of, but two or three visits are mentioned to the eastern shore.

Tiberias is on the western side, but it is towards the south. We do not know that Christ ever visited it. During his time it was a Roman colony. But just north of here lies the little plain of Gennessereth, which was one of his favorite places of resort. At that time it was very thickly peopled, and was full of towns and villages. Now it contains only one paltry village, consisting of a few houses huddled together, called Magdala. In this place Mary Magdalene was born. Josephus speaks of this plain in a very high-flown style:—

"Its nature is wonderful as well as its beauty. Its soil is so fruitful that all sorts of trees can grow upon it, and the inhabitants accordingly plant all sorts of trees there; for the temperature of the air is so well mixed that it agrees very well with those several sorts; particularly walnuts, which require the coldest air, flourish there in vast plenty. One may call this the ambition of nature, when it forces those plants which are naturally enemies to one another, to agree together. It is a happy conjunction of the seasons, as if every one laid claim to this country, for it not only nourishes different sorts of autumnal fruits beyond men's expectations, but preserves them a great while. It supplies men with the principal fruits—with grapes and figs continually during ten months of the year, and the rest of the fruits, as they become ripe, through the whole year; for, besides the good temperature of the air, it is also watered from a most fertile fountain. The people of the country call it Capernaum. The length of this country extends itself along the banks of the lake, which bears the same name, for thirty furlongs, and is in breadth twenty, and this is the nature of the place."

This is a description of the plain as it was in the time of our Saviour. It looks very different now. I could not find any walnut or olive trees. A few scattered fig trees and a few palms are all I have seen of the magnificent abundance that Josephus describes.

So much for a general description of the

lake and its shores. I will now tell you something about the different places on it which I have visited. Tell Hum is on the northwestern shore of the lake, and is said by some to mark the site of Capernaum, where our Saviour's residence seems chiefly to have been. But this is disputed by others. They say that Khan Minyeh, a little further to the south, is the place. Father and Mr. Hamilton both incline to Tell Hum. As for me, I am not capable of judging. But I very much wish there was no doubt about some of these sacred places, and especially Capernaum. It would have been delightful to me could I have felt *certain* that I was in the very place where Jesus had lived. We are sure of Bethlehem, where he was born; of Nazareth, where he passed his childhood and youth. It is strange that the town which was his residence during his ministry should be so unknown.

This city, which, in the time of Christ, was "exalted unto heaven," and which he pronounced judgment against because of its pride and wickedness, has now not only lost its place on the earth, but its name. Nobody seems to know exactly where it was. Tell Hum is now nothing but a mass of ruins, extending along the shore for half a mile. These ruins are principally foundations of buildings and loose stones.

In one place we saw very beautiful columns. The only living things we encountered among these ruins were some wretched-looking Arabs, and still more wretched-looking dogs prowling around.

There are no ruins at Khan Minyeh except the khan itself. This has been a very large building. Between it and the shore is a fountain which forms a brook, which flows into the lake. Over the fountain is a fig tree, which gives it its name—Ain-et-Tin, fountain of the fig.

Chorazin and Bethsaida have also ceased to exist. They are supposed to have been on the northern shore of the lake, near the Jordan.

We forded the river on a sand-bar near the place where it emptied into the lake. The water came up to my feet. In America we would scarcely call the Jordan a river—at that point at any rate. It is not more than eighty feet wide. In some places it is full of shoals and sand-bars, in others it is deep. The water is not clear. The banks are low and not very picturesque. But the whole of this northern end of the lake is said to be very fertile indeed, owing, no doubt, to the streams of water which flow through it, for there are several beside the Jordan.

On the eastern shore there is nothing interesting. We crossed high hills and deep, narrow wadies, until I was tired. We saw no villages, no towns, no people, except wandering Arabs, who, as I have told you so often, and now tell you again, are everywhere.

On the southern shore the country is much like the northern, and is very fertile. Both shores belong to the government, and are cultivated by the Ghawarineh. These people are Arabs, but somewhat different from the Arabs we have so long been acquainted with. These are more quiet and rather more civilized-looking, stay longer in one place, and have some idea of farming. They raise wheat, barley, millet, and Indian corn. They own large herds of cattle, among them are buffaloes. Think of buffaloes being used as beasts of burden! But I take it that these buffaloes are very different from those in our Western territories. These are much smaller and more easily tamed, but they are ill-tempered looking animals.

I saw one of the Ghawarineh ladies churning milk. A large goat-skin filled with milk is hung on a framework of sticks, and jerked violently back and forth until the butter came. Then she took it out, put it in a pan over the fire, and *melted* it. Afterward she poured it into skin bottles. I have had some experience with this butter. It is about as thick as honey now, but in the summer they say it is like oil. Whichever time you eat it it is poor, miserable stuff.

These people have strange habitations. They are tents made of mats; a poor shelter, I should think. Ibrahim tells me that these Ghawarineh are looked upon with a great deal of contempt by the Bedouins. Indeed I think Ibrahim himself has not too high an opinion of them. They are not a very interesting people, but I think them an improvement on the Bedouins.

At the southern part the lake is but three miles wide. Out of this the Jordan makes its appearance again. We found it very different from the river on the northern shore. It is very rapid, and more than a hundred feet wide. It is very shallow, not more than four and five feet deep. There was once a bridge here, but it is all broken to pieces, and the ruins partly choke up the river.

Captain Lynch, who commanded the expedition sent to the Dead Sea some years ago by the United States government, has told us all about the Jordan. They went down the river from the lake to the Dead Sea in boats. They found many rapids in the river—they shot the boats over some and carried them round others. There were no settlements on the river until they reached the town of Jericho, near the Dead Sea. The banks were very fertile, and covered with trees and brilliant flowers.

On this shore we found some precious stones—jasper, chalcedony and agate—but they were small and rough, and look very different from what they do when polished up. I have some for you. I find there are different kinds of chalcedony. That we found is the onyx, which is of a thick white color; then there is the cornelian, which is red; the sardonyx, which is striped red and white, and the chrysoprasis, which is sea-green and rare. We spent a day on the southern shore, at the special request of Hartley and myself, as we wished to have a pop at the wild fowl which we saw flying about so plentifully. Hartley had capital luck, and so had I, considering I am not much accustomed to using a gun. Beside ducks and pigeons, which we wanted, we shot other birds we did not care so much about—storks, herons, hawks and swallows. What we did not want ourselves we gave away to the ragged children who swarmed around us.

Now, at last, having gone quite round the lake, and got back to my starting-point, I will tell you something about Tiberias. It is a town of some size for this part of the world, having about two thousand inhabitants; but it is a very dirty and disagreeable place. I am glad our tents are pitched at a respectable distance from it. There is a Christian quarter and a Jewish quarter, and I really don't know which looks the worst. There is, also, a Christian church here—St. Peter's. It is not at all pretty, and is used by both Latins and Greeks. This is one of the holy cities of the Jews. They believe that Jacob resided here, and near here they expect the Messiah to appear. Jerusalem, Hebron, Safed, and Tiberias are the four holy cities of the Jews in Palestine. Some years ago this place was almost entirely destroyed by an earthquake. A thick wall which enclosed the town on the land side was thrown down. Nearly all the houses were overthrown, and six hundred persons perished. Father says this is a volcanic region, which means it is liable to earthquakes.

The hot baths near Tiberias are very famous. There is a large bathing-house, which would be quite elegant if it were not so very dirty. The building is quite handsome. The public bath is in the centre. So is a large reservoir, in a circular room. There is a marble pavement around the reservoir; steps lead from the room down to it. The roof is supported by pillars. There are four springs, but the water from them all is collected into this great reservoir. It is so hot that I could not bear my hand in it an instant. I should think it would boil an egg. And yet the basin was always full of men—Jews and Arabs—the well, the sick, the lame, the deaf, and the blind, were crowded together in this steaming place; either hoping to keep well or get cured. The water is not drinkable, being salt and bitter, with a strong taste of sulphur. But, used as a bath, it is considered a sovereign remedy for all ills. After this description, I need not tell you we did not take a bath. There are private rooms for those who can afford to pay for them; but they did not tempt us much more than the public bath.

We had thought of going up to Lake Huleh from here, but it has been decided that this is not the proper season. We are to wait till summer, and then, perhaps, we may extend our travels as far as Damascus. Father and Mr. Hamilton wish to go back to Jerusalem, so we take up our line of march for that place to-morrow. We strike across the country from here to Carmel, and travel down the sea-coast to Joppa, and from there to Jerusalem.

As we have spent several days among the

scenes where most of our Saviour's miracles were performed, and where he lived the greater part of the time he spent in preaching and doing good, we have talked a great deal about his life and character, and Hartley told me a legend about him, which is so beautiful I have written it down for you:—

"Jesus arrived one evening at the gates of a certain city, and he sent his disciples forward to prepare supper, while he himself, intent on doing good, walked through the streets into the market-place.

"And he saw at the corner of the market some people gathered together, looking at an object on the ground; and he drew near, to see what it might be. It was a dead dog, with a halter round his neck, by which he appeared to have been dragged through the dirt; and a viler, a more abject, a more unclean thing never met the eyes of man.

"And those who stood by looked on with abhorrence.

"'Faugh!' said one, 'it pollutes the air.' 'How long,' said another, 'shall this foul beast offend the sight?' 'Look at his torn hide,' said a third, 'one could not even cut a shoe out of it.' 'And his ears,' said a fourth, 'all dragged and bleeding.' 'No doubt,' said a fifth, 'he hath been hanged for thieving!'

"And Jesus heard them, and, looking down compassionately on the dead creature, he said, 'Pearls are not equal to the whiteness of his teeth!'

"Then the people turned towards him with amazement, and said among themselves, 'Who is this? It must be Jesus of Nazareth, for only he would find something to pity and approve, even in a dead dog!'

"And being ashamed, they bowed their heads before him, and each went on his way."

Your affectionate friend,

PHILIP.

XI.

JOPPA, Jan. 28, 18—.

MY DEAR HARRY:—

We have taken a wide circuit since I last wrote to you. We were then on the eve of leaving Tiberias. We were all sorry to bid good-bye to the shores of Galilee. There is no part of the Holy Lord that seems to me so full of our Saviour's presence as the country around Lake Gennessereth.

On our way from Tiberias to Samaria, we suddenly found ourselves in the midst of a great concourse of people, who were making a prodigious uproar, and we discovered we had lighted on a fair, which is held every Monday at Kahn-et-Teijar. There were thousands of people from all parts of the country, and every variety of merchandise was being sold, such as cotton, barley, wheat, Indian corn, horses, donkeys, cattle, sheep, cheese, honey, chickens, eggs, figs, raisins, shoes, ready-made clothes, jewels, nails, saddles, sacks, and goodness knows what beside! These merchants tried to drive as hard bargains as we Americans are said to do, and I know they made ten times more noise. They had no idea of order or politeness. Each man was crying his wares at the risk of breaking his windpipe; the chickens cackled; the dogs barked; the donkeys brayed; altogether there was a delightful din and confusion. I enjoyed it very much, and was glad that Ibrahim stopped. He took that occasion to lay in a supply of provisions, which is a work requiring time and patience, owing to the great desire each party always has to cheat the other.

We crossed the plain of Esdraelon, and the "ancient river Kishon." At the time we crossed the river it was of a respectable size, swollen by the winter rains, but it is often entirely dry. The idea of calling such a thing a river! Just fancy the Delaware river going dry in the summer! This river rises at the Fountain of Jenin, and flows in a northwestern direction to the base of Mount Carmel, and empties into the Mediterranean Sea. A great many streams flow into it on its course. It is famous as the scene of the battle of Barak, the sacrifice of Elijah, and the slaughter of Baal's priests.

Carmel is a beautiful mountain, and covered with trees and shrubs. It is situated on a cape, and overlooks the sea. This is not the Mount Carmel where Elijah's sacriifice was offered.

Carmel is a range of mountains, eighteen miles long, and the sacrifice took place some distance below the mountain now known particularly by the name of Carmel. We climbed it from the sea-shore. It is easy of ascent, but full of wild looking gorges and deep ravines. Its name means "vineyard of God," and in the ancient days it was celebrated for its vines. There are none there now. We were very cordially received, and kindly treated, by the brethren in the convent of Elias, which is on the very summit. In the convent they showed us a grotto, said to have been Elijah's residence; it has a beautiful marble entrance, and a chapel over it.

You have read of the Carmelites, or Barefooted Monks, who used to travel so extensively over Europe, on begging expeditions. They first came from this convent, and thus gave the name to others.

From here we had a view of the town and bay of Acre. The town is nothing but a strong fortress, and is constantly under martial law. Between us and the town I saw a river, which father told me was the Belus, where the Phœnician sailors accidentally discovered the art of making glass. You know the story, of course.

We did not make the monks a long visit, and before dark were down in our camp. The

Arabs we have now in our employ are much more lively than those we had on our former journey to Jerusalem. The cook, a good-natured, chubby fellow, seems to tell very droll stories, judging from the laughter he provokes. Ibrahim sometimes translates his jokes, but they don't seem to me very funny; but a joke is generally spoiled by translating. I was amused watching their proceedings that night, after our visit to Carmel. They were just preparing to cook their supper. The burning embers of their fire were scraped aside, and a large hole made in the heated ground, where it had been. Within this hole was laid a mass of dough, made of flour and water. They seemed to be very careful to make it fit exactly. Over this the coals were raked, and the fire again built up. A great pot of rice was then set on the fire, and, as it cooked, from time to time melted butter was poured in; the rice was stirred with the branch of a tree. When this mess was done to their liking, the pot was taken off, the fire scraped away, and the bread taken out. The bottom of the loaf was the color of the dirt it had been buried in, the top was covered with ashes and dented with cinders. The whole party gathered around the pot, and tearing off great pieces of bread, they made them into spoons, and each one kept dipping his spoon into the pot until they had had enough rice, when they went to work and eat their spoons! I thought of "pious Eneas" eating his table. Rice is the principal food of this people. They never seem to tire of it. In the meantime the Arab cook was preparing our supper, which he did very nicely, for he is a first-rate cook. Our supper consisted of the thin cakes of bread which I described to you in a former letter, some very good fried chicken, an omelette, and excellent tea. We had no butter, for none of us like the oily, rancid thing they call butter here.

After supper the Arabs gathered themselves together in a half circle, and one of their number stood forth, and, with a marvellous twisting of his body, and throwing about of his arms, began to tell a story, which all listened to with the deepest attention, and with glistening eyes. Ibrahim said it was all in poetry, and that he made it up as he went along! I felt quite proud to think we had a poet for a camel driver. When he had finished there was silence for a time, and then a young man I had never seen before made his appearance before the circle. It seems he was a wandering Arab minstrel, who had joined our camp during our absence. He had a curious musical instrument, with only one string. I cannot say much in praise of the music. Ibrahim said it was a love song. It was a tremendously long one, and the instrument and the minstrel's voice, together, sounded like the creaking of a wheelbarrow, and the howling of a dog. The lover, as is usual with them in all countries, I believe, was constantly in the deepest anguish of despair. I judge so from the music, for I could not understand the words. No one had the heart to stop this horrible performance, for these wild men enjoyed it evidently with the keenest delight. The picturesque dresses of these Arabs set off the scene, and increased the effect. I don't think I have ever described the whole costume to you. Their heads are closely shaved, and covered with a small red cap; over this they wear the turban, which is a coarse cotton shawl of gay colors, generally striped; the ends of this hang down on each side of the face, and are usually ornamented with fringe. They wear cloaks, or abas, made of camel's hair, and very coarse, with broad stripes. Beneath this they wear a long loose gown, made of cotton, either white or colored. This is fastened at the waist by a leather belt. They wear red shoes, with pointed toes. When all these things are bright and clean the effect is quite pretty, but I must confess they are generally the opposites of bright and clean.

I forgot to say that there are a dozen villages on Mount Carmel, inhabited by Moslems and Druses.

After leaving Carmel, our course lay along the sea shore most of the way to Cæsarea. As we approached this place, we rode for quite a long distance through an oak forest. This was a treat, for forests are rare in this country. In fact, I think nothing has struck me so much as the absence of trees. This is why single trees are so often mentioned in the Bible to mark places. In this country the oak is an evergreen; the branches were spreading, and the under ones very low. It was like having a green roof overhead, and between the branches we could get glimpses of the sea. They say that robbers abound in that neighborhood, but we did not see any. I believe these gentlemen are afraid of us, for we have never been assaulted by them. I do so want to have a good robber fight.

There are many ruins in and around the present Cæsarea, for, like all the other towns of this remarkable country, its glory has passed away. It was once a mighty city. These ruins are now nearly all rubbish; but there is one we visited before entering the city which still keeps some of its form and comeliness, though it has been turned into a Moslem castle. It was once an immense theatre, probably built by the Romans. The seats are all gone, but the vaults underneath are in good preservation, and are used as stables by the peasants. After leaving the theatre our road lay over an ancient aqueduct, now broken. This used to supply the city with water, but I expect no water has flowed through it for hundreds of years. It was not a very agreeable road, for it was very narrow, and had a fearful bog on one side and fathomless mud on the other. Some of the covered aqueducts are of immense size—the natives say that a man on horseback can ride through them! Perhaps so—we have no means of knowing.

This place was formerly called Strato's tower. Herod changed its name to Cæsarea. He it was who beautified it, and made of it a mighty city; so the time of its grandeur was the first century of the Christian era. Here Herod erected heathen temples and theatres, and placed great statues of idols, and in this way gave great offence to the Jews, and their quarrels became so bitter that they ended in the terrible war which concluded, as you know, by the total destruction of the whole Jewish nation. One of the very first acts of the war was the massacre of twenty thousand Jews in Cæsarea.

So much for the profane history of the city, which is full of war and cruelty. Its incidents of sacred history are full of tenderness and peace. Here Cornelius fasted and prayed, and was visited by Peter, so that here took place the first Gentile baptism. (Don't you think we Gentiles should hold Cæsarea in everlasting honor?) Here Paul was kept a prisoner for two years and preached to the rulers of the land. Here Eusebius, the historian, lived, and here Origen studied and wrote commentaries.

And yet the place is entirely deserted! Not a human being did we see in it, the day we spent there, but ourselves. At night it is inhabited by robbers.

Our camp was near the mills of Zerka. These mills are two hours' ride from Cæsarea, on the river Zerka, which, being translated, means Crocodile River. There are ten mills in operation, and near them the ruins of many more. The mill-dam is said to be very ancient. It is certainly the biggest mill-dam I ever saw. The wall is nearly six hundred feet long, and twenty feet thick. The Zerka is actually inhabited by crocodiles. So we were told, and Hartley and I stole away, and went down to the marsh where they have been seen, hoping to get a sight of one. But the great reptiles kept themselves very quiet, and perhaps it was as well, for neither of us knew much about the habits of the crocodiles, and might have found ourselves in uncomfortable quarters.

Cæsarea is in the plain of Sharon. In my mind this name is always connected with roses. When we passed over it it was not the season of roses, but Ibrahim says he never saw one there in his life. They must have all died out since Solomon's time, which is a pity.

On leaving the plain of Sharon, we left the country of the ancient Phœnicians, and entered upon the plain of Philistia—the country of the Philistines. This extends south as far as Gaza, and is exceedingly fertile, and contains immense cornfields. This plain is remarkable, in the Old Testament, for the numerous battles fought on it between the Jews and Philistines, and especially as the scene of Sampson's exploits.

In this plain, on the sea-coast, is Joppa, whose modern name is Jaffa. We were twelve hours in the saddle from Cæsarea to Jaffa, only stopping once to rest and eat dinner. It was the longest ride I had yet taken, and I was very tired. But I was up bright and early this morning, to explore this very, very old city of Joppa. It was the chief seaport of the Jews. It has been sacked, pillaged, burned, and rebuilt again and again. For the last twenty years it has been gradually increasing in population and importance. It now contains fifteen thousand inhabitants. The reasons it has lately increased are these:—1. It is the usual landing place for pilgrims, Christians, and Jews to the holy city. 2. There are great soap factories here. 3. Silk is produced in considerable quantities. 4. Fruit and corn are exported from here to Europe. All that sounds matter-of-fact and business-like enough, don't it? More like the United States than Palestine!

The main street, in fact the only one, extends along the sea-shore. It would not express the condition of things there this morning, if I told you it was crowded. It was *jammed* with people, and it was a labor to push our way through them. There were respectable citizens attending to their own business, and very busy they were. There were newly arrived pilgrims, staring about them in a distracted manner. Camels, mules, donkeys, and horses disputed the street with the human beings. But the most numerous of all objects were the Arabs and beggars—diseased, ragged, noisy, and quarrelsome creatures they were. And that reminds me that Dorcas lived in this city. She ought to be here now, with at least a hundred assistants.

We were shown the house where Simon the tanner resided. If I had only been *certain* it was his house; but it is so very doubtful.

There are two beautiful things in Jaffa. One is the building over the fountain, near the gate. There is always a crowd there, of course. The other is the orchards and gardens. They are beautiful at this season, with only the leaves on the trees; what must they be in the time of flowers and fruit? The fruits are bananas, oranges, lemons, pomegranates, apples, apricots, quinces, and plums. These orchards have to be constantly watered, because there is no dependence to be placed in the rains here. They come in floods, or not at all. The method of watering is curious and simple. All underneath the sand there seems to be water; dig where you will, you will invariably find water at no great distance. This is raised by Persian wheels. A wide cog-wheel is carried around horizontally by a mule, with a sweep. This turns a larger one perpendicularly, which is directly above the mouth of the well. Over this revolves two rough, thick ropes, made of twigs and branches twisted together, and upon them are fastened small jars, or wooden buckets. One side descends while the other rises, carrying the small buckets with them—those descending empty, those ascending full—and as they pass over the top, they are emptied into a trough which carries the water to the cistern.

Your affectionate friend,

PHILIP.

XII.

JERUSALEM, Feb. 6, 18—.

MY DEAR HARRY:—

Again in El Kuds! I am right glad to be back here once more, though I have enjoyed the journey we have taken since we left this city. As we expect to remain here now for some time, Hartley and I have fixed up our room with books, maps, pictures, curiosities and guns, and so feel very much at home. We are staying with the Fanshawes. I think it is fortunate they took such a large house.

My last letter was written from Joppa. On leaving there we turned away from the sea-coast, and took the direct road to Jerusalem. But we stopped one day in Lydda, or Lydd, or Ludd, for it has all these names. I will keep the old Bible one. It was in this village Peter was staying when he was sent for to go to Joppa, on account of the death of Dorcas. It is a pretty little place, surrounded by groves of fruit trees. It has two thousand inhabitants. The only thing in the way of antiquities which the place contains is a very large church, which is now partly in ruins. It is called the Church of St. George. About half of the church is in ruins, only scattered columns and broken arches are left. The other half is entire, but the Mohammedans have built it into a mosque, and though I am provoked with the barbarians, I must confess the mosque is very pretty, and has a very high and graceful minaret. The church is of pale yellow stone, cut from the quarries near here. This church was built by the Crusaders, probably soon after their arrival in this country. When they took Lydda from the Saracens, they found there the splendid sepulchre of St. George. The church had been levelled to the ground, but they soon built another. Whether this is the same one, or whether that was destroyed, and another erected in its place, no one seems to know. Historians disagree on this point, as it seems they do on many others. I used to think that whatever I read in history must be true, but travel has knocked that out of my head, as well as a great many other foolish notions. Since I have been in the country, I have heard so many marvellous legends about this wonderful saint, that I have tried to find out his true history. All that I have been able to learn is, that he was born in Lydda, suffered martyrdom in Nicomedia in the third century, and that his body was carried to Lydda, and buried there.

In rambling about the streets of the town, we met a marriage procession. The bride was being conducted to her future home by her husband and his friends. First came the bridegroom, with his friends walking two and two. Then a gorgeous silk canopy, under which the bride was walking, we were told, though the silk hangings hid her completely from view. On each side of this was a man with a drawn sword in his hand. Behind the canopy were a number of women, and after these followed the musicians. The music *twanged* most horribly, the men shouted, and the women screamed; it was an awful din. Perhaps the bride liked it—I hope she did—but I don't think Caroline would like to have a man with a drawn sword walking on each side of her.

It took us nearly eleven hours to ride from Lydda to Jerusalem. The first part of the way was very pleasant, but the last half was over the "hill country of Judea," and was tolerably rough, I can tell you.

I saw a very curious sight yesterday, which I will try to describe to you. Father, Hartley, and myself took a ride into the country, just for a little excursion, without any particular object. After riding some distance, through quite a pretty country, we were about to return when we espied a group of persons, round the door of a house, at the entrance to a village. We immediately rode there to inquire into matters. We were told that a serpent charmer had just gone into the house, to get a venomous serpent out of it. Hartley and I sprang from our horses, and made a rush towards the door, father following rather more slowly. On entering we found ourselves in a large room, with rough stone walls, without paint or plaster. The owners of the house had been frightened away by the serpent. Beside the serpent-charmer, there were only a few scared-looking Arabs in the room. The serpent-charmer was a dervish, and though he was very dirty, was, in spite of it, a stately looking, dignified man. He seemed pleased to have three such intelligent Franks(!) to witness his skill. Father, in a pleasant way, asked permission to search the dervish, to see if he had any perfumes, or anything concealed about him, and the man cheerfully consented. While this was going on, Hartley and I were looking for the snake. We could see no sign of it, though the room was not very light, and there were plenty of dark corners where a snake might coil himself up.

The dervish had in his hand a short stick of palm wood. This he struck against the wall three times in a very mysterious manner. Then he whistled; then made a noise with his tongue, something like the clucking of a hen; then he spit on the ground, and said, "I adjure you, by God, if ye be above, or if ye be below, that ye come forth! I adjure you by the most great name, if ye be obedient, come forth, and if ye be disobedient, die! die! die!" He then raised his arm, and pointed his stick high up the wall, close against the ceiling, and moved it slowly along. Suddenly the stick was stopped, and there glided on it a snake, ten feet long, and a very venomous one. It glided down the stick, and wound itself around the arm of the dervish, but it did not seem angry or inclined to hurt any one. The frightened Arabs ran at the very first glimpse of the snake, but the dervish, not at all alarmed, carried the snake out on his arm, and it was soon killed.

The dervish walked with us part of the way back to the city, and father, who understands Arabic well enough to hold short conversations, tried to find out the dervish's secret; but he kept talking, and told nothing, for these dervishes are very cunning.

While they were talking, a scorpion suddenly ran out into the road from under a stone. The dervish immediately began his whistling and clucking; the scorpion stopped, then ran a little way towards the dervish, and stopped again. Quick as thought the dervish stretched out his hand, and, seizing the scorpion, placed it in his bosom, in the loose folds of his dress. I expected he would be stung, for these scorpions are irritable little creatures, and sting quickly, though the cool weather might have made it somewhat torpid, as they like the very hottest weather. But the scorpion lay very quietly; he may have gone to sleep there, for aught I know, for it was lying in his bosom when we parted from him.

Is not all this very wonderful? I could scarcely have believed it if I had not seen it. Father says these charmers have been exercising their wonderful powers for hundreds of years, and he mentioned several passages in the Bible which refer to them. There are some serpents that these charmers seem to have no power over. The adder is one; the Arabs say the adder puts its tail in its ears, so that it cannot hear the charmer. This is a curious story, but it agrees with the text, which is familiar to us:—"Like the deaf adder, which stoppeth her ears, and will not hear the voice of the charmer, charm he never so wisely."

I think this serpent-charming trick would be a good thing for our wizards in America. I wonder they don't come over here and get the secret. I have no doubt it could be bought with money, for these dervishes are as fond of that article as our own magicians could possibly be.

Your affectionate friend,

PHILIP.

XIII.

JERUSALEM, March 23, 18—.

MY DEAR HARRY:—

I have allowed a longer time than usual to pass without writing to you, but I have had very little that was interesting to write about. I think I have described already all the places of interest, in and around Jerusalem. I have visited them over and over again; the Mount of Olives and Church of the Holy Sepulchre have been my favorite places of resort.

I am writing this letter on Sunday night, because I wish to send it in the mail which goes to Beirut to-morrow; that is to say, a gentleman who leaves for that place in the morning, has offered to carry letters for us, so that they can reach Europe sooner. We expect to be off by daybreak for the Jordan, therefore you must not expect a long letter to-night.

Lent is over; to-day closed the religious services for holy week. The city has been crowded all during Lent; people from every nation under heaven come here at that time. During the past week the crowd has been greater than it was before; the khans and convents are overflowing, and so are most of the private houses; and the streets have been packed with people. In a few days I expect they will all have melted away, and the streets be as quiet and deserted as they were before Lent commenced.

On Palm Sunday I was in the court in front of the Holy Sepulchre early in the morning, in order to secure a palm branch. I thought it likely it was the only time in my life that I could carry a real palm branch on Palm Sunday. There are always an immense number of palm branches piled up near the entrance to distribute. Early as it was, there was quite a crowd there, which increased to such numbers, that I was somewhat frightened. However, I got my palm branch. and when the door was opened the crowd went in in tolerable order, so I was not crushed, as I feared I would be. Inside of the church we formed in a long, solemn procession, and walked three times around the Sepulchre, holding our palm branches aloft. After this I made the best of my way out of the church, but it took me some time, for the crowd was increasing every minute. I intend always to keep my palm branch. I left the congregation celebrating high mass.

In the afternoon of Wednesday we all went

to the Church of the Holy Sepulchre, to see the foot-washing. The church was even more crowded than on Sunday. The priests were most magnificently dressed; they fairly glittered with silver and gold. Twelve monks, plainly dressed, represent the twelve apostles. A priest goes around and washes their feet from a silver basin, which is carried by a deacon; he wipes them, makes the sign of a cross on them, kisses them, and then gives to each monk a crucifix. This is in imitation of our Saviour's washing the disciples' feet. What an imitation!

On Good Friday we attended services in the English church, and heard a very good sermon from the bishop.

But yesterday, Easter eve, was the great day of the Greeks. Early in the morning we took our seats in the Frank gallery in the great Rotunda of the Church of the Holy Sepulchre. Below us, on the floor of the building, was the greatest crowd I ever saw in my life. The pilgrims were wedged together in one dense mass, or rather two dense masses, one round the sepulchre, another near the walls of the church. Between the two was a lane, formed by two circles of Turkish soldiers; I was surprised to see these, but was told they were needed to keep order, to prevent any one being crushed, and to interfere if there was any danger of the Latins and Greeks coming to blows, for disgraceful fights have taken place between these two sects in front of the sepulchre of Him who taught "peace, good will among men." Moslem soldiers keeping peace between Christians! I never expected to see such a sight as that.

For a long time, nearly three hours I should think, every thing was quiet, the people all had a look as if some great and very solemn event was about to take place; in the Greek Chapel of the sepulchre there is a little hole in the wall, and I noticed that those pilgrims near enough to it, put their hands there, and held fast to it all the time. All this time I did not feel tired; I was amused and interested in watching the people below me, and trying to find out how many different nations were represented there. I think I may safely say, every nation I ever heard of.

About noon a group of pilgrims darted out from the mass into the open lane I mentioned as running in a circle between the two crowds. Others followed them, and they began running violently around the sepulchre. This set the example, and the pilgrims poured into the lane until it was quite crowded. They ran, and jumped, and danced, and whirled round, and howled, and clapped their hands. They dressed in all sorts of costumes, even to goat skins; and some had scarcely any clothes at all. Occasionally one man would jump on another's shoulders, sometimes quite over his head, reminding me of leap-frog; sometimes a man would lift another on his back and run off with him. Of all the funny sights I ever saw, that was the funniest. I laughed until I actually cried. I did not know what to make of this whirligig at first, but after a time I could hear some words that I understood, such as: "This is the tomb of Jesus Christ!" "God save the Sultan!" "Jesus Christ has redeemed us!" and I found then it was a part of their religious ceremony.

After a couple of hours, this excitement began to subside, the runners dropped off one by one, and soon the lane was clear again. Then from the Greek Church, at the east of the rotunda, a procession made its appearance. This procession marched round the sepulchre, carrying embroidered banners. They chanted solemn and beautiful chants, but with these were soon mingled yells like those of savages, for the whole crowd of pilgrims, now greatly excited, began to scream violently. Three times the procession went round the sepulchre. At the third time, the Turkish soldiers formed into line, and fell in behind. The multitude pressed together. We could see that they were getting impatient as the time for the great event drew near. This great mass of pilgrims believe that on this day every year the Holy Ghost descends on the tomb of Christ, and appears there as a bright flame! This was the event they were now all looking for. It is thought by them that the presence of the infidel soldiers prevents the descent of the holy fire. So that, after the soldiers began to march after the procession, a grand rush was made upon them by the people. In a twinkling the procession was broken up, bishops, priests, and deacons ran for their lives, and were scattered in all directions; the banners fell and were trampled under foot, or caught up by the crowd; and the Turkish soldiers allowed themselves to be driven out of the church.

While this was going on, a small band of priests hurried the bishop who was to receive the holy fire, to the Chapel of the Sepulchre, and the door was closed on him. I expected now the crowd would be silent, but I was mistaken; the uproar was awful. From the little hole, which I have mentioned in the chapel, to the outside wall, a narrow lane was formed, and on each side of this, as far as I could see, hundreds of bare arms were stretched out, holding candles to be lighted with the sacred fire.

At last it came. A bright light appeared at the hole. Those nearest the place instantly lighted their candles; the light passed from candle to candle along the lane, and back from them among the crowd, until the whole vast building was one blaze of thousands of burning candles. The bishop was carried out of the chapel in a fainting state, to make the pilgrims believe that he was overcome by the glory. A lighted taper was given to a horseman at the door of the church, who galloped off with it to Bethlehem, to light the lamps in the Church of the Nativity, which I told you of in a former letter.

The crowd then rushed out of the church. Sometimes the pressure is so great that many lives are lost; at one time some hundreds of people were killed.

I hope that some day these ignorant pilgrims will learn a better way of keeping Easter eve. I think that the priests who teach them these things are very much to blame.

And now, as it is getting late, I will bid you "good night." I do not know where my next letter will be dated from.

Your affectionate friend,

PHILIP.

XIV.

SHORE OF THE DEAD SEA, April 4, 18—.

MY DEAR HARRY:—

Actually on the shores of the Dead Sea! Yes! I, Philip Conway, am seated on a rock by the Dead Sea, writing a letter to my friend Harry, who is in Philadelphia, probably at this time in the school-room, making allowance for the difference in time. I suppose it is somewhere about ten o'clock in that practical *new* city of schools and candy-shops, market-houses and drays. There are no such things about me. All around me would be unbroken solitude, were it not for the noise of our muleteers and soldiers, who are breaking up camp. Such an uproar you never heard, and all about nothing, for they have packed away tents, and tent-pins, and baggage so many times they ought to know exactly what to do. But, as they have just commenced operations, and, as I know by experience, it takes them a long time, I shall be able to say a good deal to you before they are done, and I have much to tell. I think you will be pleased to get a letter written on the shore of this famous sea. I have made a little arbor of green branches to protect me from the sun, which is scorching at this time. With a rock for my table, and the Dead Sea spread out before me, I feel that I shall be able to write. How many marvellous stories we have read, and believed too, about this sea! But they were not *all* true, as you will discover before you finish this letter.

Father, Mr. Hamilton, William Fanshawe, Hartley, and myself, left Jerusalem Monday after Easter. We intended to go to Jericho on that day, and the whole population of the city turned out to see us off. This will not seem strange when I tell you that several thousands of pilgrims left at the same time. Most of these belonged to the Greek Church, and were going to bathe in the river Jordan. We were glad to avail ourselves of their protection, as the region through which we were to pass was infested with very daring robbers. The Turkish governor was with us, and we were protected by a band of Turkish soldiers. Woe to the unlucky pilgrim that loitered behind or strayed away from the line! He would surely fall into the hands of thieves, and never be heard of again. Such a cavalcade as it was! A small army of about ten thousand men, women, and children; many of these latter were little babies.

A great white flag was borne aloft in front; this is the flag of the pilgrims; in the rear was the green Turkish flag. Our party was among the last of the pilgrims, and near the soldiers. I often rode out of the ranks to look at the long procession. It was a pretty sight to see it winding around the foot of the Mount of Olives, and so on to the village of Bethany. The pilgrims were mounted on a variety of animals, horses, mules, asses and camels. Sometimes a whole family would be mounted on one poor, patient camel. The soldiers' horses were all fine ones. Considering the vast number of people, they were very quiet. I thought they were almost *too* quiet. In America what a clattering of tongues there would have been, especially among so many women. After we left Bethany, I scarcely heard any sound except the trampling of thousands of animals' feet, and the horrible din of the kettle drums, which I believe never ceased. I think the drums must have been a kind of defiance to the robbers to come if they dared.

There has been a great deal said about the pilgrims going *down* to the Jordan, and, after leaving Bethany, I understood it well. For a mile or two it seemed to me we were going down what was almost a precipice, and a very rocky one, and the rocks quite slippery. Saladin had to put his dainty little feet down pretty firmly. All got down without broken limbs. When these were safely past, we still kept going down, though not quite so fast as before. The valley of the Dead Sea is nearly four thousand feet lower than Jerusalem, which fact accounts for the rapid descent we had to make.

The road was very gloomy—not a house or tree to be seen. At last we reached the plain, and in the middle of the afternoon arrived at a poor little village of about fifty houses. Here I saw the pilgrims dismounting, and scattering over the plain in various directions. I asked Mr. Hamilton why they did not keep on to Jericho? "Why this is Jericho," he said. "This Jericho!" said I; "why this is no town!' "This is Jericho, nevertheless," he replied; "no trace of the great city of ancient times remains."

The inhabitants of these huts are very much afraid either of robbers or visitors, for they have planted thorn bushes all around their houses, and the branches are so plaited and twisted together that neither horse nor man will attack them.

The tents were pitched on a barren, sandy

plain, where there was but little shade, therefore it was intolerably hot, for this is the warmest part of Palestine. We found our tent was under a fig tree, near the castle. Ibrahim is a jewel of a courier, and always manages to get the best of every thing.

This castle was built by the crusaders. There is nothing left of it but the tower, which is forty feet high. This is the only ruin in Jericho, and is a little out of the village.

After dinner our party again mounted their horses, and rode two miles in a northwesterly direction, to visit the fountain Ain-es-Sultan. This fountain rises at the foot of a small hill. It is very large, and is full of small fish. The water is very cool and sweet. But there was a time when it was not fit to drink, and Elisha made it sweet with a cruse of salt.* There is, I believe, no doubt about this being the very fountain.

Hartley and I retired early that night, as we expected to get up long before daylight; but, just as we were settling ourselves to sleep, father came and asked us if we would like to go to the top of the castle, where we would get a good view of the encampment and the river. We were not long in getting to the top of the

*2 Kings ii. 19.

tower, for the night was cloudless, and the moon being full, it was almost as light as day. Every thing was very quiet. Not a sound broke the stillness, except the songs of the bulbuls. Here and there we could see a sentinel pacing up and down, but all else in the camp was motionless. Hundreds and hundreds of tents were spread below us in every direction. Within them were sleeping men, women, and children from all nations and of all sects; Mahommedans, Druses, Maronites, Roman Catholics, Greeks, Armenians, Copts, Syrians, Episcopalians, Presbyterians, Baptists, and Methodists, all brought there by one source of interest, the river Jordan; this river made sacred by the baptism of Christ, for it is said that Christ's baptism took place at this spot. Whether this is true or not, it is believed by the whole Greek Church.

Indeed, Harry, it was a wonderful sight to behold that great city of tents spread there—a vast congregation of mixed nations and various creeds, brought together, not for warlike preparation, but to perform a ceremony which gave public testimony of their common faith in Christ. At a little distance we could see the Jordan, shining faintly in the moonlight, all unconscious of the scene which would be passing there in a few hours.

We were soon sound asleep, but it seemed to me we had been sleeping only a few minutes, when the drums beat a tremendous reveille, and started every body to their feet. I found it was three o'clock in the morning. The bathing was to be done early, so as to get through before the heat of the day. In an hour's time every body was mounted, and we took up the line of march again, towards the southeast. The soldiers rode in double ranks on each side of the pilgrims. The governor and his body-guard brought up the rear, and in front were the guards, carrying huge torches made of old rags dipped in turpentine, and stuck on the top of long poles. We reached the river bank at sunrise.

At this place the river was ten feet deep in the middle of the stream, but much shallower near the shore. The banks were steep and high, and covered with thickets of tamarisk, willows, and canes, except at the bathing-place, where there was a wide, open space. The river is very narrow. In America, we would call it a little stream. It was yellow and muddy-looking, and the current seemed to be quite rapid. This is said to be the place, not only of Christ's baptism, but also where the Israelites crossed the river when the waters divided to let them pass over on dry land. Both these points have been disputed. The Latins have a bathing-place higher up the river, where *they* say Christ was baptized.

We stood, with some hundreds of spectators, on the river-bank. Soon the pilgrims plunged in—thousands of them. Most of them wore white dresses. These are kept till they die, and used as their winding sheets. It is considered sufficient to bathe once in a lifetime, and those pilgrims who had little children with them, held them under the water a minute, as that would save them the trouble and expense of performing the pilgrimage themselves in after years. Very economical in their religion! They generally remained in the water sometime, and some seemed mightily to enjoy it. The women, many of them, were very timid, and I was afraid there would be a sad end to all this pleasure; so many people in a narrow and rapid stream; but I did not hear of a single person being drowned, though we heard it was not uncommon at these times. There was not much noise or excitement. Every body went to work as if it was a business they had made up their minds to. After the bath was over, we all returned to the camp, took dinner, and before night I believe all the pilgrims were in their tents asleep. At all events, I know I was, for the day had been very hot, and I was very tired.

At midnight the drums called us all up again, and our company mounted the tower to witness the departure of the pilgrims, for we were not to return with them. It was the grandest torchlight procession I ever saw, extending for miles and miles. It seemed like a river of light running up and down the mountains and over the plain.

It was so near morning when the last of the train departed, that we concluded to take our breakfast and start on our own journey, which was in an entirely different direction from that the pilgrims had taken. This we did accordingly, and by sunrise, had turned our faces towards the Dead Sea. And now we rode on in high state indeed; for, in addition to our courier and muleteers, we were escorted by a guard of ten Turkish soldiers. Our party was now too large and formidable to be attacked by robbers or any of the wild Arab tribes of this region. They have all kept pretty well out of our way. I am not going to bore you with a particular account of every day and hour; but will proceed to pick out the most interesting things from my memory and my note-book.

We are now, at this present writing, on the southwestern shore of the Sea, with a wilderness on one side of us and a desert on the other, a desolate-looking country behind us, and a strange, still sea before us. And yet this country used to be as "the garden of the Lord"* before the destruction of Sodom and Gomorrah. Now it is the most dreary, horrible place that one can well imagine. I don't believe it would be possible for civilized beings to live here.

Father and Mr. Hamilton have had a great desire to spend some time near this sea; but they have decided to leave now, for they find it too disagreeable in this place. They talk of returning, if we stay in the country long enough, and bringing a boat with them, leaving Hartley and me in Jerusalem; but I hope they will not do it, for it is a very unhealthy region. The Arabs call it "the Sea accursed of God," and say it is dangerous to stay long on its shores. Father considered this an Arab superstition before he came here; but I think he is getting a little uneasy himself as to the state of things. You can have no idea how offensive the air is at times; it smells like bad eggs. This odor does not come from the sea-water, but from the marshes, which are more numerous than agreeable. The heat too, has a bad effect

*Genesis xiii. 10.

upon us all. It makes us sleepy and stupid. Then there is no fresh water any where near us; what we have we brought with us from Ain Jidy. And, in addition to all the rest, every night the mosquitoes torment us almost into fits. But in spite of all these discomforts, we have so far kept in tolerable health and very good spirits.

The Dead Sea or Lake Asphaltites is forty-eight miles long, and twelve broad in the widest part. The southern part, on which we are now encamped, is the narrowest. It has a long, curiously-shaped peninsula running into it from the eastern shore. This southern sea is said to cover the two cities of Sodom and Gomorrah, though some say they are not under the sea at all, but must have been some where on the shore.

The water is intensely salt and very greasy and bitter. The least dash of spray will leave a crust of salt on you, and, when the water touches the skin, it gives you a prickly sensation. No fish, or living thing of any kind is to be found in this sea, and no wonder; nothing could live in such bitter water. The barrenness of the soil is owing to the salt which abounds here. It is deposited in great quantities on the shore. Some of the stones are beautifully encrusted with it. I have collected some fine specimens for you. It is a beautiful sight to see the dead branches of trees which have been into the water; when the wind lifts them in the air, the little crystals of salt with which they are covered sparkle and glitter in the sunlight as our Philadelphia trees do when they are covered with ice.

Almost all the trees we have seen are dead ones. Every thing looks dead. The rocks, and stones, and sand are generally of a dull, ashy hue, and what is very strange, I think, all the birds and animals we have seen are of exactly the same color. Here and there we have found patches of green, occasionally a group of trees, but no forests. Among these trees was one called the Spina Christi, or Thorn of Christ, so named, because tradition says it was from the spiny branches of this tree that the Crown of Thorns was made. We have also seen some fields of barley in the ravines. They are sown by the Arabs, but it is seldom that the same tribe that sows the grain reaps it. It falls to the lot of the most powerful.

We will not visit the eastern shore of this sea. There is nothing there of special interest, and the mountains are very steep and full of precipices. It was the country of Moab. We have travelled the whole length of the western shore. It is very rocky, in some places mountainous. Indeed, the sea is shut in on all sides by high, rocky hills. There are a great many caves in these rocks. Some of them have fine, arched doorways, and are much ornamented. These must have been used for dwellings. And these doorways were the means of leading me into a fine scrape. I had a great desire to enter one and see what I could discover, but could never find any that were not so choked with rubbish it would have been the labor of a week to have cleared one out. But one day, when I had wandered a little way from the rest, I found an open doorway, with no rubbish about it. I ought to have gone and told the others my good fortune; but I thought it would be a very brave thing to explore the cave alone. So in I marched as bold as a lion. I found myself in a large room, with a high ceiling. Having looked about me with great satisfaction, I proceeded to make the tour of the apartment, hoping to find something curious; and as the room was not very light, it was necessary to proceed slowly. Suddenly I heard a noise which made me stand still—it sounded wonderfully like teeth snapping together. I looked in that direction, and, through the darkness, I saw two flaming eyes. I found my way out of that cave very quickly. Not far from the cave I met Ibrahim and two of our valiant guard.

They went in and shot the creature, which proved to be a large panther—a beautiful animal, with a splendid spotted skin. I will show you the skin when I get home. I would not have been afraid of the panther if I had had my gun with me, of course. Its eyes would have been a good mark, and I could have killed it easily; but I had neither gun nor pistol about me. There are not many panthers here, but they are seen occasionally, and sometimes hyenas are met with. I would give a great deal to see a hyena. We have seen a good many hares, and plenty of pigeons and other birds that we do not know, all ash-colored.

It is not true that birds cannot fly over this sea. I have seen them quite often. Only a little while ago I watched one entirely across to the other shore.

You must not think that our way here from Jericho was an easy ride along the sandy beach. It was very seldom we could keep along the beach at all; but the path led us over great rocks and high hills; a very rough-and-tumble kind of riding, which I liked well enough; but Mr. Hamilton and father looked at the rocks in dismay, the muleteers quarreled and scolded, and the soldiers took everything complacently. The beach has no shells on it, of course, as there are no shell-fish in the sea.

There are two very interesting places on this shore—Ain Jidy and Masada. Ain Jidy is a beautiful green oasis in this wide desert. It is made green by a fountain of clear, fresh water. It is four hundred feet above the sea, on the side of a mountain. A good many trees grow there—among others the tree which produces gum-arabic. I wish I was a botanist, and then I could tell you the names of the beautiful flowers we saw growing there. Ain Jidy means the "fountain of goats," and, therefore, I was not surprised to see these pretty creatures scrambling over the rocks above the fountain. This is Engaddi, mentioned in the Bible. Long, long ago, there was a city there. In the caves in this neighborhood David and his followers hid from Saul and his soldiers. The Essenes—the Jewish hermits—made use of these caves long after the time of David.

Masada is on the top of a very high rock. The sides are very steep and rugged; but we determined to climb to the top, if possible. We accomplished it in about two hours, sometimes scrambling on our hands and knees. The sides of the mounatins were full of holes, which had been made in them for some purpose. We found the ruins of a fortress there. A ruined wall was all around the summit. We entered through an arched doorway carved with crosses and queer figures. Within the walls was a heap of rubbish, fragments of marble, mosaic and pottery, and nothing very valuable. There were windows in the walls in some places. Looking through one of these, we had a view of the whole sea. Below us, on a ledge of the rock, were the ruins of a tower. We could not reach it in any way. In one place we found a large room cut in the rock. The walls were stuccoed, a flight of steps led up to a gallery, which was lighted by two windows. These were all the discoveries we could make. If the rubbish was cleared away, perhaps some strange things might be brought to light. There is a curious piece of history connected with this place, to be found in Josephus. Father showed it to me, and I will write it for you:—

"When Baseus was dead, in Judea, Flavius Silva succeded him as procurator there; who, when he saw that all the rest of the country was subdued in this war, and that there was but one stronghold that was not taken, he got all his army together that lay in different places, and made an expedition against it. This fortress was called Masada. It was one Eleazer, a brave man and commander of a number of Jews, called Sicarii, who had seized upon it. These Sicarii had often treated in a barbarous and wicked manner those Jews who preferred submission to the Romans to fighting for their liberty, and consequently had not a great many friends, even among their own nation. They had seized upon the fortress of Masada because it was considered impossible to take it in any manner, so wonderful were its defences, both natural and artificial. The nature of these I will now describe.

"There was a rock, not small in circumference and very high. It was encompassed with valleys of such vast depth downward that the eye could not reach their bottoms; they were abrupt, and such as no animal could walk upon, except at the places of the rock where it subsides in order to afford a passage for ascent, though not without difficulty. Now, of the ways that led to it, one was from the Lake Asphaltites, towards the sun-rising, and another on the west, where the ascent is easier. The one of these ways was called the Serpent, as resembling that animal in its narrowness and perpetual windings, for it was broken off at the prominent precipices of the rock and returned frequently into itself, and lengthening again by

20

little and little hath much ado to proceed forward, and he who would walk along it must first go on one leg and then on the other; there was, also, nothing but destruction in case your feet slipped, for on each side there was a vasty deep chasm or precipice, sufficient to quell the courage of anybody by the terror it infused into the mind. When, therefore, a man had gone along this way for thirty furlongs, the rest was the top of the hill, not ending in a small point, but was no other than a plain upon the highest part of the mountain. Upon this top of the hill Jonathan, the high priest, first of all built a fortress, and called it Masada; after which the rebuilding of the place occupied the attention of King Herod to a great degree; he also built a wall round the entire top of the hill, seven furlongs long; it was composed of white stones; its height was twelve cubits, and the breadth eight cubits; there were also erected upon that wall thirty-eight towers, each fifty cubits high, out of which you might pass into lesser edifices, which were built on the inside round the entire wall; for the king reserved the top of the hill, which was of a fat soil and better mould than any valley for agriculture, that such as committed themselves to this fortress for their preservation might not even there be quite destitute of food, in case they should ever be in want of it from abroad. However, he built a palace therein at the western ascent; it was within and beneath the walls of the citadel, but inclined to its north side. Now the wall of this palace was very high and strong, and had at its four corners towers sixty cubits high. He also had cut many and great pits, as reservoirs for water, out of the rocks at every one of the places that were inhabited, both above and round about the palace, and before the wall; and by this contrivance he endeavored to have the water for several uses, as if there had been no fountains there. Here was also a road, dug from the palace and leading to the very top of the mountain, which yet could not be seen by those without the walls, nor, indeed, could enemies easily make use of the roads, for the road on the east side, as we have already taken notice, could not be walked on by reason of its nature; and, for the western road, he built a large tower at its narrowest place, at a thousand cubits from the top of the hill, which tower could not possibly be passed by, nor could it be easily taken, nor, indeed, could those who walked along it without any fear, such was its contrivance, easily get to the end of it.

"Within this fortress was laid up corn in great quantities, and such as would subsist men for a long time, also wine and oil in abundance, and pulse and dates heaped together. These fruits were fresh and full ripe, and no way inferior to fruits newly laid in, which Eleazer found here. These had been stored here by Herod nearly a hundred years before. There were also great quantities of weapons of war. Herod had prepared this fortress as a refuge, in case he should be deposed by the Jews or by Antony.

"Silva, having first gained the whole of the surrounding country, built a wall quite round the entire fortress, that none of the besieged should escape. He then pitched his camp and prepared to besiege the place. There was but one place that would admit of the banks he was to raise, three hundred cubits below the highest point of the rock, on a rock called the White Promontory. Here his army built up a bank of earth two hundred cubits high; this was for the support of the battering rams, catapults, and other machines for breaking down walls. There was also a tower made sixty cubits high, and all covered with plates of iron, out of which the Romans threw darts and stones from the engines, and soon made those on the walls to retire, and would not let them lift their heads above the works. This kept the Jews from getting on the walls and throwing darts, and lowering things to protect the walls against the rams, so those who worked the engines were not molested; at the same time the iron plates protected those in the tower from any injury. With some difficulty, a great battering-ram made a hole in the walls.

"But the Jews were not disheartened even by this great misfortune. They made all haste and built another wall within that, which was made soft and yielding, and capable of avoiding the heavy blows of the rams. They laid great beams of wood lengthways in rows, one close to the end of the other, and put earth between the rows. Across these they laid other beams, and so bound together those that lay lengthways. The Romans found that this wall withstood the rams. Accordingly Silva ordered that burning torches should be thrown upon it in great numbers. It soon took fire, and there being a high wind and blowing from the south it was impossible for the Jews to put the fire out, as the wind blew the flames upon them.

"When the Romans saw that the wall was consumed they rejoiced exceedingly, for they knew that placed the garrison completely at their mercy, and night being come, they put off the attack till next day and retired to rest, first setting their watch more carefully than ever before, so that none of the Jews might escape in the night.

"Eleazer, the Jewish leader, finding there was nothing else to be done in the way of defence, and that the garrison must surrender the next day or be all slain, determined to disappoint the Romans. He called the men around him, and having first told them there were no means of escape, which, indeed, they knew before, he pictured to them the sorrows which would follow their surrender—how the Romans would not be content with killing them, but would put them to death by the most horrible and cruel tortures that could be devised; and that if the garrison refused to surrender and fought until every man fell by the sword of the Romans, still there would be left their wives and helpless children to fall into the power of the couqueror, who would treat them with great indignity and cruelty, and sell them all for slaves. He then said there was but one way of avoiding all these horrors, and that was that the men should first kill their wives and children, and then destroy each other. This, he said, though it *seemed* cruel, was, in fact, being merciful and tender to their wives and little ones, for surely it was better they should be killed by the hands of those who loved them, and thus immediately and almost without pain put an end to life; whereas, if they remained alive and fell into the hands of the Romans, they must either die a slow death by torture, or be sold into slavery.

"At first the Jews were not disposed to agree to Eleazer's proposition, for they tenderly loved their wives and children; but at last, being persuaded by his arguments that it was the best that could be done under the circumstances they were in, they made arrangements for the terrible work. The husband tenderly embraced his wife and took his children in his arms and kissed them, with tears in his eyes, and then became their executioner. When the women and children were all killed, the men chose ten of their number by lot, who were to slay the rest. Then each man lay down in the midst of his dead family that the sight of them might make him willing to die, and the ten men went round and slew them all by cutting off their heads. Then the ten cast lots to see which one of their number should slay the rest. This miserable man did not shrink from his office, nor did the nine offer any resistance, for they laid down and calmly bared their necks to the stroke. The last survivor then went the rounds to see if any there were who, perchance, had not been quite killed, that he might at once put an end to their sufferings, and if any had been entirely overlooked he would despatch them. But he found none—they were all slain. He then ran himself through with his sword and fell dead. Thus perished nine hundred and sixty persons.

"Now it happened that an old woman, who was also considered a wise woman, hid herself and her five children in a cavern under ground, and they thus escaped the slaughter.

"When the Romans attacked the fortress the next day, they were surprised to see no one, and everything seemed still, like a solitude. But, after a time, the woman and children came out of an underground cavern, and, appearing on the walls, made known to the Romans what had happened; but they could not believe it until they had entered the fortress and came upon the multitude of the slain, when they wondered at the courage and the resolution of the Jews, and their immovable contempt for death, which so great a number of them had shown when they went through such an action as that was."

I have had several searches for the apples of Sodom—fair and beautiful outside, but dust and ashes within—which you and I used to talk about so often. I have not been able to find them, and I never knew of anybody who had; and so I am inclined to think there are no such apples. Once I was sure I had got them. I found a beautiful-looking fruit, very much like a small, yellow apple; but, on cutting it open, I saw nothing which looked like dust; on the contrary, a very close, thick pulp. There is a plant called "osher," by the Arabs, which, Mr. Hamilton says, is thought to bear this celebrated fruit. We have seen a good deal of this in our travels. It is a small tree, with dark-green, glossy leaves, and clusters of delicate purple flowers. This is not the season for it to be in fruit; but the Arabs tell us it bears a pretty yellow fruit, something like an apple, and when cut open is found to contain nothing but very small black seeds.

We have experienced one sirocco—a very hot wind. It sprang up suddenly towards night, blew with great violence for a few minutes, and then passed on. During the gale, the water in the sea leaped and bubbled like boiling water in a kettle. The spray flew about at a fine rate. Standing near the shore, we found ourselves covered with salt in a few minutes. Generally, the water is perfectly motionless; you can seldom see the smallest ripple on its surface. In the heat of the day, a light mist hangs over the whole sea, owing to the rapid evaporation of the water.

I must not omit to tell you that we yesterday paid a visit to Lot's wife. You know I don't mean we paid a visit to Mrs. Lot's house; but we visited the pillar of salt into which she was turned. I expected to see something like a statue of her, and wondered if I could guess from it what sort of looking woman she was. And now what do you think I saw? Why, an irregular pillar of salt—nothing but a pillar—and that forty feet high! I was so disappointed; and, between you and me, Harry, I don't believe it is Lot's wife at all. Some people say it is just possible that this may be the same pillar of salt which is mentioned in Genesis; for, as it is three thousand years since the destruction of the cities, a vast quantity of salt may have accumulated on the original pillar and raised it to its present height; but it is my opinion that Lot's wife disappeared from the earth ages ago, and that this pillar has nothing whatever to do with her. It stands on the southern shore. There is said to be a mountain of fossil salt not very far from it. The ruins of Zoar are near. This was the city to which Lot fled on being warned to leave Sodom.

"Why, an irregular pillar of salt." Page 238.

You would have laughed to have seen us bathing this morning. We bobbed about on the water like so many corks. It is impossible to sink in it; so you see there is never any danger of being drowned. I was delighted with the sport at first, but was soon glad to scramble out of the water much quicker than I got in. It pricked my skin like hot needles; and my eyes felt as if camphor had been poured in them; the water got into my mouth, and tasted like wormwood tea with salt in it, and drew my lips together like green persimmons.

Last night I sat for a long time on the shore, close to the water, and looked down, far down into the clear, green depths, hoping I might see the tops of houses, the domes of temples, and long lines of shining streets, as they say such things can be seen in some of the South American waters which cover buried cities. But then I remembered that these cities were destroyed by fire from heaven, and that probably not a vestige of them remains. I think, Harry, I never felt such a horror of sin, and such a dread of the judgments that God will surely visit upon it, as when I sat on the barren and dreary shore of this awful sea.

Do you remember a pretty song Caroline used to sing: "What are the wild waves saying?" It kept coming into my mind last night, and I repeated to myself, "What are the still waters saying?" And, in the midst of the awful stillness and desolation, I could almost fancy I could hear "the voice of the Great Creator" answering from the depths: "For I, the Lord thy God, am a jealous God, visiting the iniquity of the fathers upon the children unto the third and fourth generation of them that hate me."

But I must close now, for I see everything is prepared for departure. I will write to you again from Jerusalem, to which city we are to return by the way of Hebron.

Your affectionate friend,

PHILIP.

XV.

JERUSALEM, April 11, 18—.

MY DEAR HARRY:—

Directly after finishing my last letter, we left the shores of the Sea of Death, and travelled in a northwesterly direction towards Hebron, which was to be our first stopping-place. Nothing of any interest occurred in the way, except that I saw women grinding corn with a hand-mill. I had seen the operation before, but always at a distance. I rode up to an Arab tent, and asked for a drink of water, in order to be near the women who were grinding. There were two of them, seated on a large piece of sackcloth. They were facing each other, and each had hold of the handle, which turns the upper stone, and pulled it back and forth. It seemed to be hard work. One threw in the grain through a hole in the upper stone. There are two stones, an upper and lower, or "nether" mill-stone. Women always do this work, and some of them must be forever at it, for every time I have passed through an Arab village I have heard these mills going.

Hebron is a large town of eight thousand inhabitants. These are mostly Moslems of the most bigoted sort. A few Jews live there, but no Christians. It is well built. The houses are two stories high, and all have domes. The town is beautifully situated in the midst of luxuriant vineyards. No part of Palestine produces such fine grapes as this. I should like to be here in grape season. The Moslems are not allowed by their religion to make wine, and therefore the grapes they do not sell are dried into raisins, or boiled down into a kind of molasses, which they call *dibs.* I can testify to its goodness.

There seems to be a great many fruit trees in and around Hebron. Many of these are in blossom, and perhaps, for that reason, we saw the place under the most favorable circumstances. It seemed to me the most beautiful place we had yet seen. The whole country was one mass of flowers. Among these numerous blossoms, the prettiest, I think, were those of the pomegranate; they are of a brilliant scarlet, and shaped like little bells. The fruit ripens in October. I have eaten plenty of pomegranates this last winter, and can say they are delicious. The seeds are a beautiful, transparent red. I wonder they don't send their fruit to America; but probably it would not keep. It is of the size, and very much the shape, of an orange, and of a greenish-yellow color. But I am wandering from Hebron itself, though pomegranates may be said to be a part of it.

There is in Hebron a great trade in glass lamps, consequently there are glass factories there, and we visited one of them. I had often visited glass factories in America, and took but little interest in these. In fact, I thought them very miserable in size and appearance, and their way of working the glass is nothing to compare to ours.

Hebron, as you perhaps remember, was one of the cities of refuge. I always had an idea that they were situated on high hills; but this one is in a valley surrounded by hills. This is one of the holy cities of the Jews.

Hebron is perhaps as old as any city in the world. It has never been destroyed, like so many of the cities of Palestine. It is mentioned in the twenty-third chapter of Genesis, under the name Kirjath-Arba, and also by the name of Mamre. In this city, or near it, Abraham, Isaac, and Jacob lived and died, and here they and their wives were buried. It was one of the cities held by the Anakims.

They were driven out by Joshua, and Hebron was made a city of refuge. It was the residence of David, where he reigned seven years and a-half as King of Judah, and at this place he was annointed King of all Israel. It was here that Absalom rebelled against his father. The city is not mentioned in the New Testament.

There are two large reservoirs just outside of the town, one at the north, and the other at the south, which are very ancient. One of these it is thought must have been the pool over which the murderers of Ishbosheth were hung by David.*

It is rather curious, I think, that the Arabs call this place El Khulil, "the Friend;" they name it thus after Abraham, who, you know, is in the Bible called "the Friend of God."

But in Hebron is something more interesting than anything I have yet mentioned. This is the cave of Machpelah, which is in the side of a hill in the city. I believe that every sacred locality in Palestine but this one has been doubted by somebody, and given cause for disputes. In regard to this cave there is absolute certainty. It was purchased by Abraham for a burial place, at the time of Sarah's death.†

* 2 Samuel iv. 1. † Gen. xxiii. 19, 20.

When Jacob died, he charged his sons to carry his body to that cave and lay it there. He says: "There they buried Abraham, and Sarah, his wife; there they buried Isaac, and Rebekah, his wife; and there I buried Leah."* Jacob's request was complied with; his sons carried him from Egypt into Canaan, and buried him in the cave of Machpelah in Hebron. Father has read a great deal of history in relation to this matter, and he says it so happens that Hebron has always been in the possession of people who held the patriarchs in great reverence, and would not allow their tombs to be disturbed. Here, then, in the red-colored rock, in the hill-side, is the cave of Machpelah, and within it are the sepulchres of Abraham, Isaac, and Jacob; Sarah, Rebekah, and Leah. Over this cave the Jews built an edifice to mark the spot, and surrounded it with a high wall without windows. When this was built, is not known; some think during the reign of Solomon, and some say later; but it is mentioned by very ancient writers. But the Jews have no control over it now. It has passed into the hands of the Moslems, and they, following their usual fashion, have converted it into a mosque, and they hold the place as so sacred, that no one

* Gen. lix. 31.

is allowed to enter the building but Moslems, and no one can go into the cave except a very few of the highest among them. This has been the case for hundreds of years, and, therefore, very little is known about the cave, except some wild accounts by different travellers, which everybody is in doubt whether to believe or not. But all agree in the belief that the sepulchres are really there. Several times Hartley and myself walked round and round this building at a respectful distance, for we were not allowed to go too near, and wished for a carpet like the famous one in the Arabian Nights. We would have transported ourselves to America in a twinkling, and in a few hours we would have been back again with volunteers enough to have driven these insolent Moslems from the town, while we explored the cave. But, alas! we had no such carpet. They are not to be found, even in the East. Indeed, since I have been in Palestine, I have come to the conclusion that it would not be wrong for America and England to get up another crusade, and drive the Moslems out of this country; only we would not do the wicked and cruel things which were done in the old crusades, and we would let the Jews share in our good fortune.

The outer wall is built of large stones, and is very high. There are no windows in it.

There is a minaret at each corner, and square pilasters without capitals all around on the walls. There are two entrances, and long flights of steps lead up to the doors. Just at the left of one of these doors is a small hole cut in the wall, and through this the Jews are permitted to look inside. You will wish for some description of the inside building. Father has given me two; one is by a traveller who wrote in the twelfth century, but father says he is not always to be relied on. He says that an iron door admits you into a cave, which is empty, then you go through a second which is also empty, and in the third are six sepulchres; all with inscriptions on their lids. That on Abraham's was: "This is the sepulchre of our father Abraham, on whom be peace."

The other traveller gives a longer description; but he had not seen it himself, and wrote what he was told by those who had. "The mosque is a square building, with little external decoration. Behind it is a small cupola with eight or ten windows, beneath which is the tomb of Esau. Ascending from the street at the corner of the mosque, you pass through an arched way by a flight of steps to a wide platform, at the end of which is another short ascent. To the left is the court, out of which, to the left again, you enter the mosque. The dimensions within are about ninety feet by sixty. Immediately on the right of the door is the tomb of Sarah, and beyond it that of Abraham, having a passage between them into the court. Corresponding to these, on the opposite side of the mosque, are the tombs of Isaac and Rebekah, and behind these is a recess for prayer and a pulpit. These tombs resemble small huts, with a window on each side, and folding doors in front, the lower part of wood, and the upper of iron. Within each of these is an *imitation* of the sarcophagus, which lies in the cave below the mosque, and which no one is allowed to enter. Those seen above resemble coffins with tops like pyramids, and are covered with green silk, lettered with verses from the Koran. The doors of these tombs are left constantly open. The mosque is supported by four columns. A cord passes from the mosque into the cave below, and supports a lamp which is kept constantly burning in the cave of Machpelah, where the actual sarcophagi rest. At the upper end of the court is the chief place of prayer, and on the opposite side of the mosque are two large tombs, where are deposited the two larger sarcophagi of Jacob and Leah."

By the way, being in Hebron, made me think of the Anakims, who lived there years ago. I always had a curiosity to know just how high these giants were. The rabbis tell marvellous stories about them, which they certainly do not expect any body to believe. One of the most astonishing of these is about Og, King of Bashan. Here is a description of him: "The soles of his feet were forty miles long. The waters of the Deluge only reached to his ankles. He, being one of the antediluvian giants, escaped the general destruction, and reappeared in subsequent history as Eleazer of Damascus, Abraham's servant. Abraham, who was only the size of seventy-four ordinary men, could yet scold terribly. Under his rebuke, Eleazer trembled so violently, that one of his double teeth dropped out, and this the patriarch had made into an ivory bedstead, and ever after slept on it. When Moses, who was ten ells high, fought with this giant, who was then Og, King of Bashan, he seized an axe ten ells long, and jumped ten ells high, and struck with all his might, and hit the giant on the ankle." Rabbi Jochanan says: "I have been a gravedigger, and once, when I was chasing a roe, it fled into a shin-bone, I ran after it, and followed it for three miles, but could neither overtake it, nor see any end to the shin-bone; so I returned, and was told that this was the shinbone of Og, King of Bashan."

We were in Hebron two days, and, on the

afternoon of the second day, we had a little picnic under the great oak, which is two miles from Hebron, in a northwesterly direction. I have mentioned before that there are but few large trees in this country; therefore, wherever there is one, it is famous, and this oak is perhaps the most famous in the country. It is very old—nobody knows how old—the inhabitants of the region believe it was there in the time of Abraham; in fact, that it is the very oak under which he entertained the two angels.* This idea, of course, is absurd. But it is called "The oak of Father Abraham." It is a fine, evergreen oak, twenty-six feet in circumference near the ground, and its branches extend over ground nearly three hundred feet in circumference. Under the tree the grass was soft and green, and we all thought it a delightful place. Some distance beyond the oak is an unfinished house, which we went to look at. Nobody could tell us who commenced building it, or when. Whoever began it, intended it to be strong, for the stones are large and thick. It is called "the House of Abraham," for no reason that I could discover, except that it was near the place where Abraham lived.

We stopped for a few hours at Tekoa. This

*Genesis xviii. 4.

was the birth-place of the prophet Amos,* and Joab called a wise woman from here to plead in behalf of Absalom.† There are some ruins there, but they are not of much interest. The place and the country around it were entirely deserted. We visited the cave of Adullam, which is near Tekoa. At last we entered a cave, said to be the cave of Adullam, where David and his followers lived most of the time that Saul was hunting for him.‡ That cave was somewhere in this neighborhood, and this would have been a very good one for their purpose. The cave contained several large chambers and winding passages, and our guide told us we could easily get lost in it. It was very dark indeed; our torches only made it more awful and gloomy. We had a great deal of trouble getting to it and back again, but I rather liked the fun of that. We had to slide down rocks, jump over chasms, and walk along shelves of rocks which overhung precipices. Father thought the cave was not worth the journey.

After leaving Tekoa, we took a roundabout course to Jerusalem, in order that we might visit Mar Saba. We passed through the valley of Urtas—Wady Urtas you will see it marked on the map. In this wady are three great

* Amos i. 1. † 2 Sam. xiv. 2. ‡ 1 Sam. xxii. 1.

reservoirs, called El Burak and the Pools of Solomon. They were built by that king to convey water to Jerusalem. The aqueducts are broken, and, therefore, useless; but the cisterns are in very good order. They were all nearly full of water when I saw them. The water comes from a fountain at a little distance. These cisterns are built of great square stones, and are of immense size. To tell you that the largest one was six hundred feet long, two hundred wide, and fifty deep, would not give you any idea of it; but perhaps you may imagine it when I tell you that, when full, it would float the largest-sized man-of-war.

It was harvest time, and all through the valley they were gathering in the grain and threshing it. Father and Mr. Hamilton said the wheat was of very fine quality. I don't know anything about that; but I will tell you how they thresh it. They tie the wheat into sheaves, as we do, in the fields. These sheaves are put upon the backs of little donkeys, who are then driven to the threshing-floors. The donkeys are so heavily loaded, that generally you can see nothing of them but their little legs. The threshing-floors are circular places, marked out on the ground, and in these circles the earth is beaten down until it is very hard. The grain is spread out upon it and trodden out by animals. The grain is then tossed up in the air; the wind carries away the chaff, and the wheat falls to the ground by its own weight. It is a slow process and a very wasteful one. Wheat machines should be introduced into this country. The harvest is not thus early everywhere in Palestine, only in the warm valleys near the Dead Sea.

Mar Saba is the most curious place I ever saw in my life. It is a convent built *into* the sides of a precipice. The cells of the monks are in the ledges, cut out of solid rock. I don't know what to compare the convent to, unless it may be an immensely high set of book-shelves, with rows of cells instead of books. That part of the valley of the Kedron in which it is situated is a very wild and romantic spot. We arrived at the narrow valley in the afternoon. At the entrance of the valley we came upon a tower and stopped before its door. But we were not admitted immediately, by any means. A tin case was let down to us by a rope. In this father placed the letter of introduction we had from the Greek convent at Jerusalem; the tin case was then drawn up. I suppose the monks found it all right, for we were soon after admitted. We were conducted through a long passage and up some steps into the parlor. Here we were politely received by a kind-looking old monk, who invited us to stay all night, which invitation we accepted. The old monk offered us bread, and coffee, and raisins; and afterward we were shown to our rooms, which were a row of cells. The first thing I did was to climb to the roof of mine. I found myself on a ledge of rock about one-third of the way up the precipice. Above me were layers of cells, rising one upon another until it made me dizzy to look at them. On the opposite side of the narrow valley was another precipice, also full of little cells. I found these cliffs had other inmates besides the monks; these were hawks, which were flying about over my head. There were also buildings in the rocks. There was the church, with a dome and towers on it; and a little chapel, also with a dome; and the high tower at the corner. Then there was the tiniest little garden, with a few vegetables and flowers in it.

After resting and taking a bath, we were shown over the whole convent, and it was quite a tiresome journey, up and down so many steps. There are seventy cells in all. The convent contains a number of cisterns, which were full of rain water. Of course we visited the church, which was very small, but very gorgeous, being gilded and silvered, and the walls covered with pictures. I did not admire these at all, and the only one I recollect represented the massacre of fourteen thousand monks by the Saracens. The prettiest thing in the church was the pavement, which was of various colored marbles. Near the altar were two clocks, and two large, handsome chandeliers and strings of ostrich eggs. Opposite the church is a little chapel, so small that not more than half a dozen people can get into it at a time. In this is the tomb of St. Saba. The pavement between the church and chapel covers the vault for the dead. We were also shown into a room containing three hundred skulls piled up against the walls. These once belonged to the monks of St. Saba, who were killed by Chosroes, king of Persia, in the sixth century. There are not more than fifty monks there now; these are mostly Greeks. They seemed to be very simple-hearted, kind old men. I liked them very much; but I don't see the use of their shutting themselves up in that lonely place. It is said they are very kind to the Arabs, who, in times of scarcity, often go there for food. They are certainly very pleasant to travellers—that is, to gentlemen. They are so ungallant, they will not admit ladies inside the convent. If any lady travellers are benighted there, they have rooms in the tower.

The reason the monks live in such a fortress-like place, and are so cautious about admitting strangers, is from fear of the wandering Arabs. For, though the convent is but six miles from Jerusalem, it is on the borders of the region where the Bedouins are most numerous and savage.

You will be curious to know who St. Saba was. All that I can learn about him is, that he lived in the sixth century, that he was a very wise man, and, I believe, a very good one, in his way. He scooped out a cell in this rock, and other hermits followed his example, until, finally, the precipice became a convent.

We had a very good supper and breakfast at the convent, and then came to Jerusalem, where we had a cordial welcome from our friends. In a few days we leave, to return here no more.

Your affectionate friend,

PHILIP.

XVI.

HASBEIYA, June 10, 18—.

MY DEAR HARRY:—

In the middle of May we bade good-bye to the Holy City. I was sorry to part with the friends who had been so very kind to us, and I was sorry to leave Jerusalem. It is not a pleasant city. In truth, it is rather gloomy. I don't like its narrow, dirty streets, its confined air, and, more than all, I dislike the Moslems being masters there. I don't think it would be an agreeable place to live in, but then there is so much that makes one feel as if it was not such a hard matter to be good there as it is every where else; it seems, too, as if the hills all loved our Saviour's memory, and held it in reverence, and as if the stones were ready to tell beautiful things about Christ. I cannot describe my feelings; but I would like to stay there a year, and visit all its interesting places again and again.

As far as the Sea of Galilee, we passed over very nearly the same route that we did before, so I will not describe the places to you again.

The scenes were somewhat different though, for we found the whole country beautiful with flowers, busy with harvesters, and alive with great flocks of sheep.

I have said nothing to you yet about sheep and shepherds. I have seen them occasionally during the winter watching their flocks, but not in the numbers I saw in my last journey to Galilee. These shepherds are the real, old-fashioned, picturesque-looking ones, always carrying the shepherd's crook—a long stick bent into a hook at one end. They seem to look upon their sheep and lambs as so many children to be cared for. They never leave them by night or by day. During the day they lead them from place to place, wherever they may find the best pasture. At night they sleep surrounded by the flock. The shepherd always goes before; the sheep follow him. They know the voice of their own shepherd, and, if he calls to them, they instantly obey him; but they will not obey the voice of a stranger. We tried them often, but they always knew the voice of their own shepherd, and would run away from a strange voice. Some sheep always keep near the shepherd; these are his favorites, and each has a name to which it answers when called. But in a large flock many go rambling off, and then the shepherd speaks to them sharply and scolds them; sometimes a straggler gets lost, and then the wild beasts seize it. If a lamb gets sick or tired, the shepherd will carry it in his bosom, or lead it gently along.

These shepherds had dogs to help them keep the flock from straying, and, I am sorry to say, they were very mean-looking ones. The sheep-folds are called marahs. They are low, flat buildings, with large yards, which are enclosed by stone walls. Sharp thorns are planted on these to keep wild beasts from climbing over them, but the leopard and panther sometimes leap over the walls, and then the shepherd has a tough battle before him.

Don't all these things remind you of the Bible accounts of sheep and shepherds? They have remained unchanged for three thousand years.

We stopped one day at our old camp-ground at Tiberias, had some fine fishing, and then started for Lake Merom, or the Huleh. This lake is the source of the Jordan. We wished to follow the river from the Sea of Galilee, but found this was impossible, from the nature of the country. The roads we travelled were very bad.

We encamped at Safed, and looked about us a little. This town was entirely destroyed by an earthquake in 1837, so that all the houses are new. It seemed like a thriving place, more so than most of the towns in this region. There are about five thousand inhabitants, most of them Jews. This is one of their holy cities. It is on a high hill, or mountain it might be called, and the highest point of this is the real attraction of Safed. There is part of a castle there built by the crusaders. The earthquake nearly destroyed it. The castle is not of much consequence; the view is very extensive. You can see the plains and Sea of Galilee, and a long stretch of sea-coast in the distance. You can see Gilead, Bashan, Samaria, and Carmel, and the long range of the Lebanon Mountains, with the high, snowy head of Hermon. The crusaders had good taste to build a castle here, but I suspect the height and safety of the place were more in their mind than beautiful views. A great many years ago there was at Safed a Jewish school, which was very famous and produced a great many learned men. There was a printing press there, and many books were printed. It seems wonderful that such things should ever have been there. A fair is held at Safed every Friday, but we were not there on that day. Its olive orchards and vineyards were very luxuriant.

We encamped for two days near the Huleh,

and rode about the country, and up the hills, and wandered among the marshes wherever it was possible to go. Taking one of the high hills near the lake for a stand-point, we got a pretty good idea of this part of Northern Palestine. As for you, you will have to trace it all out on the map.

You will see that the river Hasbany rises in the Mountains of Lebanon, near the foot of Hermon, in the great fountain of Finarr. It flows in a southerly direction to the marshes of the Huleh, where the Leddan and Baniasy flow into it. These three rivers united form the Jordan, which may therefore be said to rise in the Huleh, though the source of the Hasbany and of the Baniasy have both been called the source of the Jordan. Of these rivers, we are told that the Hasbany is the longest, the Leddan the widest, and the Baniasy the most beautiful. The Jordan empties into Lake Huleh, but before reaching the lake, many smaller streams flow into it. On leaving Lake Huleh, the river flows southwardly to the Sea of Galilee. We could trace it nearly all the way, or at least the valley through which it flows, with the eye. [After leaving the Sea of Galilee, you know, it is a larger and more important river, and flows still in a southerly direction, the whole length of Palestine, until it is finally lost in the Dead Sea.]

Lake Huleh, as you will see, tapers nearly to a point at the south end. At the north, it is six miles wide. It is only eight miles long. The ground immediately around the lake is low, and sometimes marshy. On the north side there is a very large marsh, in many places impenetrable on account of the thick growth of bushes and briars. The land is fertile and pretty well cultivated. Wheat and barley are raised here; also large crops of Indian corn and rice. Butter is made here, and honey gathered in large quantities. Bees were to be seen every where, and there were plenty of flowers for them to feed on. The bee-hives are made of basket-work, shaped like cylinders, and covered over with mud. They are piled one above another in the form of a pyramid, and the whole is roofed with straw, or covered with a mat. The honey is very delicious. The land is cultivated by Arab farmers. It is strange to think of Arab farmers, but we have met with them in different parts of the country. They live in villages, but these villages usually have not a single house in them. They are built of tents, and are, in fact, nothing but permanent encampments. These Arab farmers are called fellahs, and a number of them are called fellahin. They are despised by the Bedouin Arabs, who roam from place to place, and the fellahs stand in great fear of their Bedouin relations. For often the Bedouins come down in force on the poor fellahs, and carry off their corn or flocks, and leave them with nothing after all their labors.

Here we saw buffaloes in abundance. I never saw any American buffaloes, but I think these must have been smaller. They are large animals, but not the monsters I have always imagined buffaloes to be. These were not very fierce-looking; they are used as cattle, and the milk is made into butter. They seemed to be fond of bathing, and it was amusing to watch their awkward gambols. They look best when galloping at full speed.

There are said to be many wild animals in the mountains around the lake, panthers and leopards, bears, wolves, jackals, hyenas, and foxes, wild boars and gazelles. We did not see any of these while at the lake. We *heard* the jackals prowling around at night and howling near the camp. We have often heard them before, for they abound in this country. I have seen them, too; they are fierce-looking beasts; they are something like dogs, but more like wolves. They feed upon carrion, but will attack small animals, and even children, when they are very hungry.

The whole lake was alive with water-fowl. It is strange there are no hunters about here. Father thought it was wrong to shoot them merely for sport; perhaps it was, but Hartley and I have had so few opportunities for trying our skill, that a chance like this was not to be lost. We killed a great many, some of which were cooked and eaten; but the greater number had to be thrown away. We were very careful not to shoot bulbuls (Asiatic nightingales), for they have sung us to sleep every night for months, and are to us dear little friends. They are beautiful birds, in shape like our kingfishers; their plumage is a rich brown, with here and there a dash of bright blue; they have deep-scarlet bills. If the bulbuls made the night delicious at Lake Huleh, the rooks and crows made day hideous; there were vast armies of them. They are sensible birds, and their wise looks and grave manners were very amusing to us. One day, firing into a colony of ducks, I killed a pelican. It was a a large, odd-looking bird, with its long, broad bill, and great splay feet. From its neck hung a great bag, in which it carries its young in times of danger. You know this bird is said to feed its young with its own blood, and, though Hartley says it is all a fable, still the bird must love its young exceedingly, or the fable never would have been told of it. I felt sorry I had shot it, for how did I know but its young might be pining for it then?

There were cane-brakes on these swamps as thick and impenetrable as those on the Mississippi River. One kind of cane had a tuft on the top of the stalk very much like broom corn, only larger and more beautiful.

As for flowers, there were myriads of them. Tell Caroline that I found there white and yellow daisies, white and scarlet anemones, oleanders and morning-glories. Then there were a great variety of lovely flowers whose names I did not know. There was a yellow flower, which grew in heavy tufts, and a crimson flower, which grew up into a long spire, like a miniature church-steeple on fire. The flower that I admired the most I was told was called the Huleh lily; it was very large, pure white, and shaped like our fleur-de-lis. As for the oleanders, words cannot describe their beauty. All along the route from Jerusalem, every river and little stream ran through banks of oleanders. You, who have only seen this plant in boxes in America, can form no idea of its exceeding luxuriance and beauty in this soft Syrian climate.

Among the birds, I forgot to mention storks, and they should be remembered, for they had so little fear of us. They would stalk directly past us with great majesty, and looked so full of stupid vanity that I was quite entertained.

Lake Huleh is the Merom of the Bible. An old tradition makes it the land of Uz, the home of Job. Many bloody battles have been fought on its hills and mountains. It was here that Abraham fought the men who conquered Sodom and carried away Lot. It was here the Israelites, under the command of Joshua, overcame the Canaanites The city of Laish lay on the north of the lake; it was destroyed by the Danites; men, women and children were slain, and the Danites rebuilt the city and named it Dan. It was the northernmost city of Palestine. There is not even the remnant of a city there now. Not far off was Abel, which Joab beseiged because Bichri was harbored there; a wise woman had Bichri's head thrown over the wall to Joab, when he raised the seige. This is now a mean little village.

There were several "mazars," or holy places of the Arabs, near the lake; but we did not visit them. One is said to be the tomb of Joshua; another, of one of the sons of Jacob.

They all had white domes over them, according to the fashion of the country.

On the northwest of the lake is the fountain of El Mellahah. The water is a little salt and slightly warm, and crowded full of fish. Did it never strike you how often I have mentioned fountains in my letters? They are certainly very numerous; the country is well watered, and father says there is no reason why Palestine should not be one of the most productive countries in the world.

From the fountain of Mellahah a short ride up the mountain took us to Kudes. This is a small village, and we did not stop there. This was one of the cities of refuge—Kadesh Naphtali. It was a great city. Barak was born there.

Only one incident occurred from there to Hasbeiya. We have not killed any gazelles; they are such pretty, timid-looking creatures, that we had not the heart to do it. But on that day the imp of mischief put it into Hartley's head to fire at a full-grown one which he saw cantering along at some distance. The distance was too great, he only wounded it; and it was brought to us, its soft, black eyes looking at us in the most pitiful manner. I had only time to glance at it, when Ibrahim said "Look there!" He was pointing to the east of a mountain not very far from where we were standing, and there, with its bright stripes showing distinctly against the clear, blue sky, stood a tiger! Hartley's gun had roused it, I suppose, and it was, no doubt, looking to see what that strange noise meant. For a minute it stood there, looking grand and savage, and then, with a bound, disappeared from our sight. Everybody was so astonished, that no one thought of firing at him; but I doubt whether we could have got good aim, he was so far. I am very glad I saw him. Tigers are very rarely seen as far north as this—this one must have wandered from the Dead Sea. As for the poor gazelle, that was killed to put it out of its misery.

Hasbeiya is a beautiful city, most pleasantly situated in a valley. It lies at the foot of Jebel-esh-Sheikh, on the western side. This is the Arab name of this mountain, so called because it is the highest among the mountains of Lebanon, being nine thousand feet high. But I prefer the old name—Hermon. So you see that at last we have reached that mountain I have been seeing from nearly all parts of the country, and have so often mentioned to you. The top is always covered with snow; or, rather, the valleys which run down the sides, are full of snow; at a distance this gives it the appearance of having radiant points, like a star. I would like to climb old Hermon, but father will not hear of it.

This is a thriving place, I believe. The valley is small, but full of fruit trees and vineyards. All kinds of religion seem to flourish here. There is a Moslem quarter, a Jewish quarter, and a Protestant quarter. It is an American missionary station; and, I believe, the church and school are in a prosperous condition. At Sidon, at Jerusalem, and here, are the only places we have been able to attend Protestant worship. Generally, on Sunday, we have had religious services in a tent, father or Mr. Hamilton officiating as ministers.

Hasbeiya also boasts of a great man—a Moslem prince—an Emir he is called, and he lives in a palace. The Emir I have not had the pleasure of seeing, but I can tell him his palace is not much to boast of in the way of beauty.

We have visited the fountain which is the source of the Hasbany. It sends forth a large volume of water, and we found there what I am sure none of us expected to see—a mill! You cannot see the fountain itself, because of the mill-dam built just below it; but you can see the water bubbling up above the dam. We rode to the bitumen pits, half a mile beyond the fountain, which are quite wonderful in their way. The pits look like small wells; some are fifty feet deep. There are as many as thirty of these pits. The bitumen is drawn up by means of a windlass. It is hard, and is said to be of the finest quality; but I could not hear of any use that was made of it, except to mix with oil to put on grape-vines, to kill the insects.

Hasbeiya, you will see, lies in the valley of Cœlo Syria, which is a long valley running between Lebanon and Ante Lebanon. Several rivers run through this valley, but the longest is the Litany. It rises near Baalbek, flows the whole length of the valley, nearly in the centre of it, and, after leaving the valley, runs in a westerly direction and empties into the Mediterranean. We crossed it in going from Sidon to Tyre, and I think I mentioned it in my letter written at that time. The river is one hundred and twenty miles long, and the scenery is said to be magnificent.

Hartley, Ibrahim and I made an excursion to this river, and spent a whole day on its banks. Mr. Hamilton was sick, and father did not go. When tired of rambling about, we sat down on a ledge of a high rock and looked down at the river, eight hundred feet below us. It was curious to watch its course—now creeping quietly along between smooth rocks, then suddenly whirling round a corner or dashing up against a precipice. We crept down to a lower ledge of the rock, and sat quite silent for a long time. I was thinking of the different places and people I had seen, and also of my far-away home. I thought of you, and wished you were with me in that romantic spot. I don't know what Hartley was thinking of; but we were so still, that the the conies crept out of the rocks near us. They look somewhat like rabbits, and have soft, dark fur; they are shy little creatures. Presently there was a great whirring and whizzing, and the conies suddenly vanished. The new comers were a pair of eagles. They came so near us, were so tremendously large, and had such fierce eyes, that I actually was afraid of them. They took no notice of us, but flew up to the rocks overhead; very likely they had an eyrie there. Hartley wished for a gun, but concluded, afterwards, he was glad he did not have it; for what good would an eagle have been to him, and he could not have it stuffed? We saw a great many afterwards; there must have been thousands about those cliffs.

I think we must have walked four or five miles, altogether, along the banks, and everywhere found them wild and rocky. I gathered pinks, altheas, snap-dragons, and many other flowers.

We have remained at Hasbeiya ten days, on account of the illness of Mr. Hamilton. We intended visiting Banias before coming to this place; but he felt so unwell when we left Huleh, that we came directly here. He is again quite well, and we will leave for Damascus to-morrow.

Father, Hartley and myself, escorted by Ibrahim only, went over to Banias one day and returned the next. The road was hilly, but tolerably good. The valleys were full of oleanders and all sorts of flowers.

Banias is called Cæsarea Philippi in the Bible. There is not much to say about the town itself. It is nothing but a poor village, in a little valley among the mountains, on the southern side of Hermon. The wonders of Banias are the castle and the fountain. The castle is two miles from Banias, on the top of a high hill. It is, in fact, a fortress, with four or five acres of ground with its walls. It is very, very old; the wisest cannot tell when it was built. It was used by the Crusaders, and also by the Saracens. Some of the towers have Christian, and some Saracenic inscriptions on them, telling who built them. We were a long time rambling over this castle. In the open space within the walls crops of tobacco were growing, and a few huts were there, in which the farmers lived. We went up the towers, and down the dark stairway into the vaults beneath, where we did not care to stay long. This staircase does not stop at these vaults, but continues on down the rock; it was all choked with rubbish, but it is believed, in the neighborhood, to lead to the fountain, two miles distant. Quite doubtful, I should think. Strange to say, nobody knows anything about the history of this castle before the Crusades, and it was considered an ancient building then!

Stumbling among the rocks, we scared out some scorpions, which luckily ran away. They are disgusting-looking reptiles. They sting with their tails; the wound is painful, but does not produce death. We were afraid they would get into our tents at night, but they were not out in sufficient force for that. In very warm weather they abound in this neighborhood.

The fountain is the source of the Baniasy. It flows out of a cavern, which is now partly choked up with stones and rubbish—the ruins of some building which formerly stood there. The water gushes out from among these great stones with a loud noise. On the rock of the cavern is an inscription in Greek, stating that there was once a temple to the god Pan at this place. Its ancient name of Panium was in honor of this god. Perhaps the great stones were part of this heathen temple. This fountain is generally called the source of the Jordan, though the fountain of the Hasbany might be called so with greater truth, for it is the longer river.

Father says it is probable that our Saviour often visited Banias and drank of its fountain. In his time it was quite a large place. The wretched houses of the present village are built among its ruins: in one place you will see a high wall, with a little hut behind it; in another place a little hovel will be perched on a heap of ruins, looking like a mouse on a flour-barrel. The country all around there is very romantic, and famed for the wild beauty of its scenery. It is also very rich and fertile, which is, perhaps, of equal consequence.

I can send this letter to Beirut by one of the missionaries who is going there, and has kindly offered to execute any commissions for us. I shall write to you again at Damascus, but don't know whether I can send a letter from there.

We are going to pass through wild regions now. We go to Damascus by the shortest route, which is over the Lebanon Mountains, north of Hermon. I don't know how long we will stay at Damascus; ther we go up the country to Baalbek; then across Lebanon again to the "Cedars;" then down the mountains to Beirut.

And now I must go to bed, and get a good night's sleep as a preparation.

Your affectionate friend,

PHILIP.

XVII.

DAMASCUS, June 30, 18—.

MY DEAR HARRY:—

We came here by the shortest route from Hasbeiya, as I told you in my last letter we intended to do. Our mountain journey, though made delightful by beautiful and romantic scenery, had very little that I could put into a letter. We did not go to the top of old Hermon, but climbed some respectable mountain peaks for all that. It was curious to notice the difference in vegetation as we went up. In the valleys we found valerian, oleanders, broom plant, &c.; a little higher up we came upon heath and ferns, and at the top of the mountain we could only gather moss. The air was cold and bracing up there. I was sorry when, from a mountain peak, I first got sight of Damascus, although it was a beautiful sight to see. But I had not had enough of the mountains.

On the spot where I had my first view of the city, the prophet Mahommed, then a camel-driver, had also his first sight of it. He was urged to enter the city, but refused, saying: "Man can have but one paradise, and my paradise is fixed above."

You may know, from this high-flown speech, that Damascus, and the approach to it, are considered very beautiful. For half an hour before reaching the city, we rode through avenues of fruit trees. There are mud walls built along the sides of the avenues. The fruit orchards are well watered by canals, cut in different directions from the Barada River. It rises among the Anti-Lebanon Mountains, flows in a south-easterly direction, and empties into a lake east of Damascus. The Awaj is a smaller river, also in the plain. These are the "Abana and Pharpar, rivers of Damascus."*

The population of the city is one hundred and fifty thousand. About half of these are Moslems. There are a good many Christians and Jews here. A wall surrounds the city, which is four miles in circumference. This has been built in modern times; the old city was much smaller. Part of the old wall still remains, and may be seen running through the middle of the city. The streets are generally narrow, crooked, and very dirty. They have the gutter in the middle of the street, like other

* 2 Kings v. 12.

Syrian cities. But the principal street is nearly straight, and goes from one side of the city to the other. It is a very busy street, and has different names in different parts; but the Christians regard it as "the street which is called Straight," in which St. Paul lived.* Many of the streets are closed by gates; these are shut an hour and a half after sunset, but a little money opens them quite easily. I believe there are between thirty and forty gates in the walls.

From the street, the houses do not appear to be handsome. They are built of wood or hard clay. I have been inside of two or three private houses, and they were exactly my ideal of Eastern houses, though I have seen none of them until now. In the centre is a court, filled with fragrant flowers and tempting fruits. In the midst of these a fountain sends up a jet of water, which falls into a marble basin and dashes the spray in every direction. From this a tank leads the water off through the garden, thus making a little brook. The house is built around this garden, and has, therefore, four sides. These have open porches on the lower floor. The rooms are all of good size. The reception-hall has a marble floor, and there is a

* Acts ix. 11.

fountain in the middle of the room. All around the walls of the rooms were passages from the Bible, in the houses I was in. The Moslems have verses from the Koran on their walls. I can't say that I much liked this fashion. It is pleasant to step from the street into one of these houses; the air is made cool by the fountains, and fragrant by the flowers.

There are numerous khans here, which are quite handsome. The one we are in is a splendid affair; quite a palace. It has a very large dome on the top. It is very well filled; all the guests are men, and most of them merchants. We have a very pleasant time here, as you may know by our staying two weeks.

As many as eighty mosques lift their domes and minarets above the houses, and give the city a beautiful appearance. There are some Jewish synagogues and a few Christian churches, both Roman Catholic and Protestant.

Many things seem to be manufactured here; among others, silk goods, but they are not so celebrated as they once were. But the name, Damask, taken from the name of this place, is still given to goods manufactured in other countries. I inquired about Damascus sword-blades, but could not hear of any place where they were made.

It is amusing to watch the trains arrive in this city. Not as they come to our cities in the West—a big locomotive puffing along, drawing a train of carriages after it. No, indeed! these trains are long lines of camels. They stalk along in what I suppose they intend to be a very imposing manner, with all kinds of merchandise in huge piles on their patient backs. The hotels are the depots of these slow-moving trains.

There are hospitals in various parts of the city; one especially for lepers; another in a beautiful plain outside the city, called "The Merj" (meadow), intended for pilgrims on their way to Mecca.

We have had several pleasant excursions from the city. One of the curiosities near here is a monstrous plane tree, which measures twenty-nine feet in circumference.

We visited the very ancient castle, but I did not care much about it. I would rather have gone into the great mosque of Ommiades, which is said to be a magnificent affair; but Christians are not allowed to enter it. I wonder what harm they think we can do their mosques. This one was built for a pagan temple, and dedicated to Juno; then it became a Christian church, consecrated by the name of St. John the Baptist. The most sacred portion of the mosque, the Moslems say, contains the head of John the Baptist.

The dogs here are positive nuisances. The streets are full of mean-looking curs, who have no master, but live entirely in the streets. They all know each other, and, if a strange dog shows himself for a minute in the streets, the whole troop will attack him. They do not trouble people, except by being forever in the way.

I think, if you were here, you would enjoy the bath as much as I do. I did not like it at first; now I think it delightful. The one we frequent is built in the Chinese style. First, you enter the rotunda, which has divans all around the walls, sufficient to accomodate sixty people. It has a domed ceiling, painted sky-blue. The walls are ornamented with Chinese pictures, done in their usual style of art. If you make known your wish to take a bath, you will be conducted into an apartment so filled with hot vapor, that it will be a couple of minutes before you will be able to distinguish any thing in the room. You will then find that it has a domed roof, with glass windows all around it; a marble floor, which is so heated that you have to have wooden clogs, three or four inches high, put on your feet before you go into the room. In the room are fountains of hot and cold water, and alabaster reservoirs. You have to sit by one of the fountains until you are partly boiled; then yellow Chinese, with shaven skulls, rub you with hands not very gentle, and made rougher by wearing horsehair gloves. Then they will lead you into a room still hotter, where you will be boiled a little more, lathered, and then thoroughly washed. By this time, if you are new to the business, you will be pretty well exhausted. You have clean, cool linen wound round you, which feels very grateful to you; a turban is coiled round the head, and you are gently supported to another room, where you sink down upon a soft couch, and have coffee or sherbet brought you.

The quarter of the city oftenest favored with my presence, contains the bazaars. Each trade here is separated from the others; the goldsmiths in one place, tailors in another, druggists in another, &c. In one place you see nothing but pipes; in another, a great variety of glass lamps. You pass through whole lanes of confectionery, which is very good, I can tell you. These bazaars remind one of the old Arcade in Philadelphia; they are built much in the same way. But the noise that reigns in these walks is entirely beyond description or comparison. The invariable rule with the merchant is to ask a great deal more for what he sells than it is worth. It is the buyer's business to beat him down to the very lowest possible price. The one that can talk the loudest wins the battle; and, as the bazaars are all in one part of the city, you may imagine the confusion of tongues. It sometimes takes a merchant a half-hour to sell a skein of thread.

On the banks of the Barada, which flows through the northwestern part of the city, are several coffee-houses. Every evening we go to one of these; sit in a balcony overhanging the river, eat ices, sip sherbet, and listen to the story-tellers. That is, Ibrahim listens and interprets, and we listen to him. They are not very good stories, and are much alike; about geniis, gnomes, and fairies, and their wonderful deeds. Sometimes the story-tellers would relate parables. These were rather better. Here is one I wrote for you, as it was rather curious, I thought.

"A wise man from Europe visited the flower-land of Damascus. When he departed to return to his native shore, he bore carefully away with him a little palm tree. He planted it in rich soil, on a sunny slope, where only the softest winds murmured. It grew up a tall, graceful shaft, and the heart of the wise man was pleased when it put forth a plume of broad, green leaves. But, as year followed year, much he marvelled that neither fruit nor flower appeared on the tree. He did not know it was pining for its Syrian sky, and only lifted its languid leaves when the east wind brought with it the fragrance of the orange groves of Damascus. Then it would throw out its arms imploringly to the wind, which only whispered softly, 'Farewell!' and went away. It had to live, and the duty of its life was to grow; so the grand head was lifted on a taller shaft, and the leaves grew broader and longer. It was a weary task to the pining palm; and the fair head drooped, and the leaves hung listless and still. But the wise man only saw a palm tree, which grew luxuriantly, and was fair to the sight.

"In the moon of roses there came a Syrian bulbul to the palm tree. Whether the east wind drove it across the sea, or whether Allah had compassion on the palm, mortal may never know; but she thrilled with joy, such as she had not known since last she heard that song on Syria's golden plains. The wise man heard the notes, and, turning on his couch, said, 'It is sweet!' He did not know a bird from heaven was outside his lattice. But the bulbul would not stay. She remembered that her mate was calling her to the Syrian shore; and before the dawning, she spread her wings, and flew towards the sea.

"To the palm the bird had brought deliverance. Its song was like the strains the muezzins sing while the day is dying. The memories of her Syrian home stirred so strong within her, that the life current ceased to flow; the palm drew her roots away from the foreign soil; she lifted her leaves but once more, laid them on the wings of the east wind, and, with a sigh of gladness, died. The wise man found a worm at the root of his palm. He said the worm had killed it. It was pitiful! his beautiful palm!

"Most unhappy is the life of the exile from Damascus. Death is not so great a punishment as this."

You will see from this letter, that I am leading a very idle life. It is a fact, but we don't stay here long, and I don't think my native energy will be killed in so short a time. Even Mr. Hamilton, who you know, is a very enterprising and active man, says no one can help yielding to the delights of Damascus. Father says if he should spend a year here, he would never want to go away; and Hartley, who is always extravagant in his remarks, says that no one who has not been to Damascus knows what enjoyment is—that in America, life is a necessity; here it is a luxury. I have not quite got hold of his idea yet. The truth is, we would all like to stay here some time if we could, but Hartley and I have to return to America—he to study medicine, and I to go to school.

Your affectionate friend,

PHILIP.

XVIII.

BEIRUT, July 11, 18—.

MY DEAR HARRY:—

We arrived here this morning, and to-morrow afternoon we will take the steamer for Alexandria. From there we go directly home by way of Italy, Germany and England. We will not stay in Europe any longer than necessary, for father says I must not lose any more time from school. I can travel in Europe when I leave college.

Our journey from Damascus to Baalbek was through wild mountain scenery, and the great numbers of ruins scattered everywhere through this wilderness, showing that a powerful nation had perished from the land, gave me a strange feeling—a sort of an idea that it was not much matter what you did in this life, for men and their works are so soon forgotten. Nobody could tell me anything about the ruins we saw; there they were, fast crumbling into dust, but the race of men, whoever they might have been, that raised those great buildings, which were to make them remembered forever, have crumbled into dust ages ago, and no one even knows their names. For this reason I did not take any interest in these ruins. I like to look at broken columns and tumble-down walls, if there is any piece of history connected with them, because then I please myself thinking of the men and women who lived there, and looked at the same stones, and I wonder what they thought, and felt, and did. But a mere pile of stones I care nothing about.

But, when we reached Baalbek, I found the ruins so perfect in parts, and so wonderful in size, that they were interesting in themselves. It is a city of ruins. They meet you everywhere. We found a good many people there. Among the ruins were some Moslem huts; on a plain near by were a number of dark camel's-hair Arab tents. Near the "public square," were pitched the white tents of a party of English travellers. Our tents were in the court of the great temple itself, which furnished us with perpetual shade. Most of the English travellers were artists, I should judge, for I could never go anywhere without finding a man perched on a stone, with paper and pencil in hand.

Nobody can form any idea of the grandeur and beauty of the buildings until he has seen them. They are said, by those whose taste in such matters is not to be questioned, to exceed in size, grace and elegance, any building or ruin in any part of the world. They are all built of white limestone, which was quarried from the hills near there. The most wonderful of these buildings is the Great Temple. On the eastern front are the remains of a large portico, one hundred and eighty feet long; at each end is a square tower. The portico is twenty feet above the ground, and once a flight of steps led up to it, but these have all disappeared. This portico had twelve columns in front, but only the pedestals of them are left. They were twelve feet in circumference. A wide hall leads from the portico into the first court, which has eight sides. It is two hundred feet long, and two hundred and fifty wide. A hall fifty feet wide leads from this into the Great Quadrangle or Court. This room is four hundred and forty feet long, and three hundred and seventy wide. A good-sized room, that! These are the most important rooms, but there are many smaller ones; small compared to these, that is to say. Some of these rooms contain columns. Fronting upon the Great Quadrangle was the "Peristyle," nearly three hundred feet long, and one hundred and sixty broad. Around

25

this was fifty-four columns. These are twenty-one feet in circumference. We used to think the pillars at Girard College were large; but, Harry, I tell you they are babies compared to these. They are seventy-six feet high. They are very beautiful, and the capitals are richly sculptured. I have written as if the fifty-four columns still remained upright. Alas! all but six have fallen, and lie there broken and covered with rubbish. These six lofty columns can be seen from all directions around Baalbek, and they are the ones we always see in pictures of that place. You remember them, I am sure. Three men, with arms extended, can just reach around one of these columns.

The Lesser Temple is not far from the other. It is two hundred and twenty-five feet long, and one hundred and twenty wide. It had thirty-four columns around it, which were forty feet high. Nineteen of these are standing. Above the columns was a cornice, made of great stones, beautifully sculptured. There are figures of gods still supported in the air by the columns, but most of the sculptures have fallen. The portal has a great many beautiful sculptures. There is a figure of an eagle, with a crest; from his beak the strings of long garlands extend on each side; the other ends are borne up by flying genii.

It is not easy to get inside of these temples, because the steps are all gone, and there is so much rubbish. And such rubbish! great shafts of broken columns, and beautiful cornices and ceilings.

We visited the quarries, which are a mile from the temples. Some stones lie there now just as they were cut—I don't know how many hundred years ago. One stone is famous for its great size. It is sixty-eight feet long, seventeen wide, and fourteen high. Three good-sized rooms might be cut in it! I asked father how they could carry such a stone a mile, and then lift it up to the top of one of those high columns? He told me that question had puzzled wiser heads than his or mine.

Near the two temples I have mentioned there is a small one, called "The Temple of the Wind." It is a graceful, circular building, almost covered with green vines and little bushes. It has eight columns.

Of course you would like to know who built these temples. I rather think, Harry, a great many people in this world are in the same predicament. If I could only tell them I should become a great man at once. Nothing is known with absolute certainty. It is generally believed that the foundations, and parts of the buildings, were built by King Solomon.

The Moslems say they were. It is evident that many different nations had a share in building them. It is pretty evident that they were dedicated to the worship of the Sun, and, in ancient times, the city bore the name of Heliopolis (City of the Sun).

A little out of the town is what I call the "public square." It is a common, shaded by walnut trees; little streams flow through it, for it is, in fact, the source of the river Leontes. It is a charming spot. I call it the "public square," because all the inhabitants of Baalbek used to collect there in the afternoon, and gossip and lounge under the trees. It was so pleasant at Baalbek, we staid there three days instead of one.

On your map of Palestine you will see a spot in the Lebanon mountains marked "Cedars." After leaving Baalbek, we made direct for that place; that is, as direct as the roads and the nature of the country would permit. We found that the part of the Cœlo Syrian valley we crossed was not so thickly settled as that lower down, towards Hermon.

The "Cedars" are remarkable, because they are the *real* cedars of Lebanon, so often mentioned in the Bible. There is only this one grove of cedar trees in all the Lebanon mountains. The oldest ones are said to be three thousand years old! We spent a night and part of a day in the grove. There are several hundred trees, old and young, large and small. Some of the trees, not the very oldest, are very graceful and beautiful. They spread out wide branches at the bottom, very near the ground; the branches grow smaller and smaller to the very top, thus making the tree into the shape of a cone; a great mass of delicate, dark green leaves. The oldest trees have several trunks, and their branches straggle rather wildly about. Large, smooth spots are cut in these trunks, where travellers have written their names. I think it is shameful, for it helps to destroy the trees. The grove is on the highest part of this range of mountains, being six thousand feet above the sea. It is in a little valley, with the tall peaks of the mountains, covered with snow, all around it. Besides these trees there is not a green thing to be seen anywhere. It is a clear grove, with no underbrush. I never saw any place I would like better to spend a summer.

There is a little Maronite chapel in this grove, and monks and other persons were living there during the summer. We bought some little articles of them, made of the cedar wood. We also got some cones, which are very large and fine, and some nuts, or seeds, which I intend to plant when I get home. The seeds have been carried from this grove to all parts of the world, and it is said there are more cedars of Lebanon within fifty miles of London than in all Syria. And yet there was a time when these mountains were covered with cedars. It was a valuable and costly wood, and was used by all the ancient nations in building their temples and public edifices. Forest after forest was cut down, until the mountains were fairly stripped of them. But they are said to grow quickly, and to be easily propagated in this climate. A good government, that took an interest in the matter, could soon cover Lebanon with cedar forests.

All the Scripture writers appear to have admired this tree very much, and compare beauful and glorious things to them. It was used in the ornamental work of Solomon's temple.

The grove, and the river near it, are considered sacred by the Syrians.

We were four days making the journey from the Cedars to Beirut. Our route lay along the western side of the Lebanon Mountains. It was very perilous in some places; but, thanks to a kind Providence, we are safely over it; and, indeed, it was charming. I don't believe there can be lovelier scenery in the world than is to be found on these mountains.

You find *something* at every turn; villages, perched up in the air; towns, snug in little valleys; old castles, where you *fancy* wonderful adventures; old convents, where you *hear* them; flocks and picturesque shepherds on the green hill-sides; Arab encampments, with their dark tents; roaring rivers; deep precipices; and, every little while, you find yourself on some high peak, where you get a magnificent view of the sea. My journey in Northern Syria is stored away, never to be forgotten. I am glad we went to Baalbek and the Cedars. They were not in the plan father had marked out for his journey. He had only intended to visit Palestine proper—the part actually occupied by the Israelites. We left that when we departed from Lake Huleh. But Lebanon always *seems* like a part of Palestine, it is so constantly mentioned in the Bible; and then you can see its snowy peaks from all Northern Palestine.

We have now made the circuit of the whole country, and seen its principal objects of interest. All Syria is not quite as large as the State of Pennsylvania. It would hardly take us as long to go over that State. We would be carried by steam there, and not by camels and donkeys; and then we would not want to stop so long over everything as one feels like doing in

Palestine. Almost every house and tree here has a story at least two thousand years old.

We bade farewell to our camels this morning, and never expect to travel with any again. I have been greatly disappointed in the disposition and manners of the camel. I thought they were meek and patient animals, suffering all things with a contented mind. They are very stupid, tolerably vicious, and the most complaining creatures I ever met with. From the moment they are made to kneel down to receive their loads they begin to growl, nor do they stop until the last package is put on. They will not endure the heavy loads that the little donkeys carry. I have several times seen them attack their drivers in a very vicious manner. They are very easily frightened, and very silly; when alarmed at any little thing they run and huddle together like sheep. They are awkward and uncouth-looking, and more solemn than the gravest judges; even the young have no sprightliness and playfulness. They seem to have very little feeling for themselves, or for each other. But I will not be too hard on the poor camels. What desert travellers would do without them I am sure I cannot tell. Their feet have soft cushions on them, which prevents them from feeling the heat of the sand, and enables them to press lightly on the loose gravel. They eat but little, and consider the thistles and thorny shrubs to be found in the desert delicious food. They can travel for days without drinking, and do not appear to suffer. They travel slowly, but never seem to get tired; they look as fresh, nearly, at the end of a day's march, as in the beginning. They are also good beasts for the mountains; their step is sure—they never slip or stumble. Their skins are so tough that they don't mind blows, unless they are very heavy. The poor creature certainly gets enough of them. If they were more gently treated, and better attended to, I have no doubt they would be better tempered and more sprightly. They kneel down to receive their loads, and when they wish to rest. They are not good beasts to ride; the motion is like that of a ship rolling in a heavy sea, and gives me the same kind of feeling. So much for the "djemmel." They have been our companions so long that I could not let them go without a parting word.

Ibrahim left us this afternoon. He appeared to be in great grief, but was consoled by some presents. He will forget us long before we will him. He has been an excellent guide and good company; always in a good humor; always willing to oblige. I hope he will have the pleasure of guiding many travellers through the Holy Land, and retire, at last, with a snug fortune.

To-morrow I must say good-bye to my pretty Saladin. I have given him to Mrs. Fanshawe, and he will be sent to Jerusalem in the morning. I wanted very much to take him home, but father says it is impossible. My only consolation is, that he will be in good hands and well cared for.

In a couple of months I shall be with you, when I can tell you many adventures, not set down in these letters.

Your affectionate friend,

PHILIP.

THE END.

www.ingramcontent.com/pod-product-compliance
Lightning Source LLC
LaVergne TN
LVHW020239110826
845151LV00003B/971

* 9 7 8 1 4 2 5 5 2 9 7 2 7 *